It's another Quality Book from CGP

This book is for anyone doing AQA Modular GCSE Maths at Foundation Level, with a predicted grade of D or below.
(If you're not sure what your predicted grade is, your teacher will be able to tell you.)

All the important topics are explained in a clear, straightforward way to help you get all the marks you can in the exam.

And of course, there are some daft bits to make the whole thing vaguely entertaining for you.

What CGP is all about

Our sole aim here at CGP is to produce the highest quality books — carefully written, immaculately presented and dangerously close to being funny.

Then we work our socks off to get them out to you — at the cheapest possible prices.

Published by CGP

Written by Richard Parsons

Updated by: Helena Hayes, Ali Palin, Caley Simpson, Janet West, Dawn Wright.

With thanks to Paul Jordin for the proofreading.

ISBN: 978 1 84762 639 4

Groovy website: www.cgpbooks.co.uk
Printed by Elanders Ltd, Newcastle upon Tyne.
Jolly bits of clipart from CorelDRAW®

Contents

Calculating Tips

Ah, the wonderful world of GCSE Maths. OK — maybe it's more like smelly socks at times. GCSE Maths is tested by three exams — yuk. Here are some tricks that could get you marks in all your exams. Read on...

Don't Be Scared of Wordy Questions

For the 'real-life' questions you've first got to work out what the question's asking you to do.

1) READ the question carefully.
   Think what bit of maths you might need to answer it.
2) Underline the BITS YOU NEED to answer the question — you might not have to use all the numbers they give you.
3) Write out the question IN MATHS and answer it, showing all your working clearly.

Example 1: A return car journey from Carlisle to Manchester uses $\frac{4}{7}$ of a tank of petrol. It costs £56 for a full tank of petrol. How much does the journey cost?

It doesn't matter where they're driving from and to.

1) The "$\frac{4}{7}$" tells you it's a fractions question.
2) Underline £56 (the cost of a full tank) and $\frac{4}{7}$ (the fraction of the tank used).
3) You want to know $\frac{4}{7}$ of £56, so in maths:
   $\frac{4}{7} \times £56 = £32$

Don't forget the units — this is a question about cost in pounds, so the units will be £.

Fractions questions are covered on page 7.

Example 2: The journey from Carlisle to Manchester (a distance of 120 miles) takes Claire 2 hours to drive. What was her average speed for this journey?

1) You're asked to find the speed, so write down the formula:
   Speed = Distance ÷ Time. (See page 85.)
2) Underline 120 miles (the distance) and 2 hours (the time taken).
3) Put the numbers in the formula:
   Speed = 120 miles ÷ 2 hours = 60 miles per hour = 60 mph

The units for speed depend on the units used for distance and time — in this case miles and hours give a speed in miles per hour (mph).

Calculating Tips

BODMAS

Brackets, Other, Division, Multiplication, Addition, Subtraction

BODMAS tells you the ORDER in which things should be done in a question:
Work out the bits in Brackets first, then Other things like squaring,
then Divide / Multiply groups of numbers before Adding or Subtracting them.

Example: Work out: $(7 - 4)^2 + 4 \times 3 \div 2$

Work it out in stages :

$= 3^2 + 4 \times 3 \div 2$	• Brackets first
$= 9 + 4 \times 3 \div 2$	• Other (squared)
$= 9 + 6$	• Multiply and Divide
$= 15$	• Add and Subtract

Money

You deal with money A LOT in real life — and you get exam questions about it.
The main things to watch out for are units (pounds and pence) and decimal places.

Example: Jennie puts £60 into a savings account which pays 1% interest at the end of a year. How much interest does she earn at the end of the year in a) pounds, and b) pence?

1) This percentages question is asking you to find 1% of £60.

2) In maths speak this means: $\frac{1}{100} \times £60 = 0.6$. (See page 8.)
The important bit now is working out what 0.6 means.

3) The question uses pounds (£60), so 0.6 means 0.6 pounds.
But answers in pounds should ALWAYS be given to TWO DECIMAL PLACES.
This might mean filling the 2nd decimal place with a zero, like this: £0.60.

You might have to round things too. E.g. £0.729 would be rounded to £0.73 so there are only 2 decimal places.

4) Part b) asks for the answer in pence.
£1 = 100p, so to change pounds into pence we TIMES BY 100:
$0.60 \times 100 = 60$p. (See page 36.)

5) So the answers are a) **£0.60**, and b) **60p**.

There's more on how to add and subtract with money on page 35.

Calculating Tips

Calculators

You're allowed to use a calculator for Units 1 and 3 — hurray! Make sure you know how your shiny grey friend can help you.

SHIFT (OR 2ND FUNC)

Press this first if you want to use something written ABOVE a button (e.g. the pi (π) button).

THE ANSWER

Before you jot down 3.6, think about what it means. E.g. in a money question, it might mean £3.60.

FRACTIONS

E.g. for $\frac{1}{4}$ press:

[1] [a b/c] [4].

For $1\frac{3}{5}$ press:

[1] [a b/c] [3] [a b/c] [5].

To cancel down a fraction, enter it and press [=].

(If you have a button that looks like [▭/▭] instead, use it in the same way.)

Pressing the [a b/c] or [S⇔D] button also switches an answer between a fraction and a decimal.

SQUARE, CUBE AND ROOTS

E.g:

[√] [9] gives the square root of 9 = 3.

[4] [x^2] gives 4 squared = 16.

[2] [x^3] gives 2 cubed = 8.

[∛] [27] gives the cube root of 27 = 3.

(See pages 43-44.)

MEMORY (STO, RCL & M+)

E.g. for $\frac{840}{15 + 12 \times 8}$:

Press [15] [+] [12] [×] [8] [=] and then [STO] [M+] to store the bottom line in the memory.

Then press [840] [÷] [RCL] [M+] [=], and the answer is 7.57.

BRACKETS

Calculators use BODMAS (see previous page), so if there's part of a question you want the calculator to do FIRST then put brackets in to tell it so.

PI (π)

(See page 74.)

The calculator stores the number for pi (= 3.142...). If it's above another button as shown here, press the [shift] button first.

The 'Ans' button brings back the number you got when you last pressed the '=' button, so you can use it like the memory buttons.

Calculating Tips

Don't Reach Straight for the Calculator

You really need to get used to WRITING DOWN YOUR WORKING OUT.

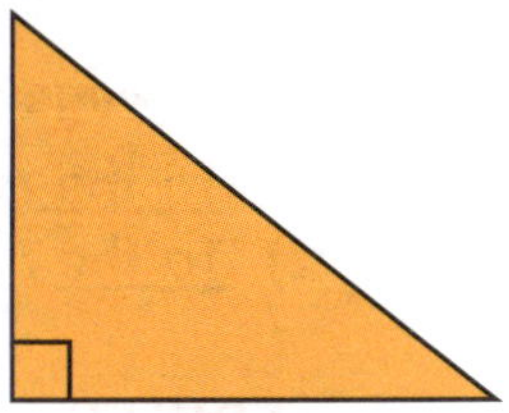

Look at these two answers to this question:
"Find the area of the triangle on the right [3 marks]."

ANSWER 1: ~~~~ 20 ✗

ANSWER 1 gets NO MARKS — 20 is wrong and there's nothing else to give marks for.

ANSWER 2: $A = \frac{1}{2} \times B \times H$ ✓
$= \frac{1}{2} \times 5 \times 4$ ✓
$= 20\ cm^2$ ✗

ANSWER 2 gets 2 MARKS — so even though the answer's wrong it still gets most of the marks!

See page 73 for how to find the area of a triangle.

Make Sure You Include the Units

Whatever the question is about, there's an important thing to remember:

ALWAYS CHECK WHETHER YOUR ANSWER NEEDS A UNIT

The question might already say what units the answer needs to be in, or you might need to work it out for yourself.

EXAMPLES:

- If you have to find an area, and the lengths are in cm, then put cm^2 at the end of the answer.
- If you have to find a volume, and the lengths are in m, then put m^3 at the end of the answer.

Learn these four pages, store, then recall...

Learn this stuff — it can really help you whichever exam you're doing. Right then, on with the rest of the show. Ladies and gentlemen — I give you the one, the only — Maths G C S Eeee.

Rounding

Big numbers and decimals are often rounded off in real life. This isn't too bad if you learn the rules.

Rounding Numbers

A decimal number is just a number with a decimal point in it.

The main ways to round off a number are:

1) 'To the nearest WHOLE NUMBER'
2) 'To the nearest TEN'
3) 'To the nearest HUNDRED'
4) 'To the nearest THOUSAND'

The 2 RULES for rounding are:

1) The number always lies between 2 POSSIBLE ANSWERS. Just choose the one it's NEAREST TO.
2) If the number is exactly in the MIDDLE, then ROUND IT UP.

EXAMPLES:

1) Give 231 to the nearest TEN.

ANSWER: 231 is between 230 and 240, but it is nearer to 230

2) Give 145 to the nearest HUNDRED.

ANSWER: 145 is between 100 and 200, but it is nearer to 100

3) Round 45.7 to the nearest WHOLE NUMBER.

ANSWER: 45.7 is between 45 and 46, but it is nearer to 46

4) Round 4500 to the nearest THOUSAND.

ANSWER: 4500 is between 4000 and 5000. In fact it is exactly halfway between them. So we ROUND IT UP (see Rule 2 above) to 5000

Decimal Places (D.P.)

There's more on decimal places on page 33.

Rounding off to ONE DECIMAL PLACE (or 1 d.p.) means leaving one digit after the decimal point. Follow the same rules as above but think carefully about the 'two possible answers'.

EXAMPLES: Round off 2.34 to 1 decimal place. ANSWER: 2.34 is between 2.3 and 2.4, but it's nearer to 2.3

Round off 4.57 to 1 decimal place. ANSWER: 4.57 is between 4.5 and 4.6, but nearer to 4.6

Round off 2.01 to 1 decimal place. ANSWER: 2.01 is between 2.0 and 2.1, but nearer to 2.0

You still have to include the zero, otherwise it's not rounded to 1 d.p.

Exam cheat wish #23 — all marks are rounded up to the nearest 100%...

Learn the 2 rules for rounding and how to round to one decimal place. Simples.

1) Round these off to the nearest whole number: a) 3.4 b) 5.2 c) 1.84 d) 6.9 e) 3.26
2) Round these numbers off to the nearest hundred: a) 286 b) 450 c) 123
3) Round these to 1 d.p: a) 5.37 b) 0.103

Fractions

Fractions are a way of showing a proportion (or part) of something. This page is all about how to deal with them. Make sure that you can do everything explained here. Every last bit.

Equivalent Fractions

$\frac{1}{4}$ ...is equivalent to... $\frac{4}{16}$

1) Equivalent fractions are equal in size...
2) ...but the numbers on the top and bottom are different.
3) To get from one fraction to an equivalent one — MULTIPLY top and bottom by the SAME NUMBER:

$$\frac{1}{2} \xrightarrow{\times 3} = \frac{3}{6} \qquad \frac{3}{4} \xrightarrow{\times 5} = \frac{15}{20} \qquad \frac{1}{5} \xrightarrow{\times 100} = \frac{100}{500}$$

Cancelling Down

1) You sometimes need to simplify a fraction by 'cancelling down'.
2) This means DIVIDING top and bottom by the SAME NUMBER.
3) To get the fraction as simple as possible, you might have to do this more than once:

$$\frac{3}{15} \xrightarrow{\div 3} = \frac{1}{5}$$

$$\frac{20}{40} \xrightarrow{\div 10} = \frac{2}{4} \xrightarrow{\div 2} = \frac{1}{2}$$

Finding a Fraction of Something — Just Multiply then Divide

1) Multiply the 'something' by the TOP of the fraction (called the numerator)...
2) ...then divide it by the BOTTOM (called the denominator).

E.g. $\frac{9}{20}$ of £360 = £360 × 9 ÷ 20 = £162

In other words, £162 is $\frac{9}{20}$ of £360.

LIGHTS... CAMERA... FRACTION...

Have a go at these questions on cancelling down and finding fractions of numbers.

1) Cancel these down as far as possible: a) $\frac{30}{36}$ b) $\frac{18}{27}$ 2) Find: a) $\frac{2}{5}$ of 50 b) $\frac{3}{8}$ of 96

Percentages

Percentages are another way of showing a proportion of something. They crop up all the time in real life — and they're bound to be in the exam. There are two important details to remember:

1) 'Per cent' (%) means 'out of 100',
   e.g. 20% means '20 out of 100' = $\frac{20}{100}$
2) 'OF' means 'times' ('×')
   e.g. 20% of £60 = $\frac{20}{100}$ × £60

'Percentage Of' Questions

E.g. "Find 20% of £60."

This is the method to use if you have a calculator:

1) WRITE IT DOWN: Find 20% of £60.

2) TRANSLATE INTO MATHS: $\frac{20}{100} \times 60$

3) WORK IT OUT: 20 ÷ 100 × 60 = £12

Percentages Without a Calculator

If you don't have a calculator, you can do it this way:

E.g. "Find 20% of £60."

1) FIND 10% BY ÷ 10: £60 ÷ 10 = £6

Look at page 37 for help with this.

2) MULTIPLY TO GET THE RIGHT %:
20% is 2 × 10%
10% is £6 (from above)
So 20% is 2 × £6 = £12

1) This way also works for things like 5% — just find 10% then halve the answer (divide by 2).
2) For something like 35% — find 30% (3 lots of 10%) and 5% (half of 10%) and add them up.
3) For small percentages, find 1% first then multiply:

E.g. "Find 6% of £500."

1) FIND 1% BY ÷ 100: £500 ÷ 100 = £5

This is on page 37 too.

2) MULTIPLY TO GET THE RIGHT %:
6% is 6 × 1%
1% is £5 (from above)
So 6% is 6 × £5 = £30

Percentages

% Discount and % Interest

1) You might see questions about discounts (money off things you buy) or interest (money that the bank can give you on your savings, or charge you on a debt).
2) There's an extra bit to these sorts of questions.
3) First find the 'percentage of', then you have to ADD IT ON (for interest or increase questions) or TAKE IT AWAY (for discount or decrease questions).

Example 1 — % Discount

In the sale, a jacket which usually costs £65 has a discount of 20%. Find the reduced price of the jacket.

ANSWER:

1) First find 20% of £65 using one of the methods from the last page:

   1) 20% of £65
   2) $\frac{20}{100} \times 65$
   3) 20 ÷ 100 × 65 = = £13

2) This is the DISCOUNT so we take it away to get the final answer: £65 – £13 = £52

Example 2 — % Interest

A bank pays 2% interest on top of £350 in a savings account. How much money is there in total?

ANSWER:

1) First find 2% of £350 using one of the methods from the last page:

   1) 2% of £350
   2) $\frac{2}{100} \times 350$
   3) 2 ÷ 100 × 350 = £7

2) This £7 is the INTEREST so we add it to the £350 to give the total: £350 + £7 = £357

It's impossible to give 110% — but that doesn't mean you shouldn't try...

Whether you're allowed a calculator or not, here are two good methods to learn to find a percentage. If the question is like the ones on this page, don't forget to add or subtract to get your final answer.

1) Find the new cost of a £30 dress which has 10% off in the sale.

Percentages

In the exam you might be asked to compare two numbers using percentages. Wowsers. Luckily, that's what this page is all about.

Comparing Numbers using Percentages

The other type of percentage question to watch for looks like this:

Give 'one number' AS A PERCENTAGE OF 'another number'

EXAMPLE: "Express £2 as a percentage of £20."

This is the method to use:

Fraction		Decimal		Percentage
$\frac{2}{20}$	$2 \div 20$ →	0.1	$\times 100$ →	10%
1) First make a FRACTION out of the two numbers, always with the smaller number on top.		2) DIVIDE them to get a DECIMAL.		3) Then multiply by 100 to get a PERCENTAGE.

Example:

"In a sale, a £60 tennis racket has £12 off. By what PERCENTAGE has it been reduced?"

So this is asking you to give £12 as a percentage of £60.

ANSWER: The two numbers you want to compare are the REDUCTION (which is £12) and the ORIGINAL VALUE (which is £60). Then use the method shown above:

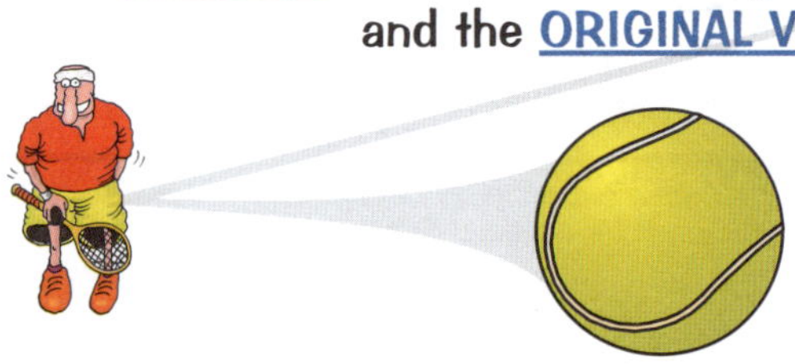

Fraction → Decimal → Percentage:

$\frac{12}{60}$ → 0.2 → 20%

So the tennis racket has been reduced by 20%.

63% of all statistics are made up...

Yep, percentages really do pop up everywhere. Time to check what you've learnt from this page...

1) A house increases in value by £28 000, from £140 000.
   What is the increase in value of the house as a percentage?

Ratios

A ratio is a way of comparing amounts. E.g. if there are girls and boys in the ratio 3:4, it means for every 3 girls, there are 4 boys.

Here's how to write ratios and simplify them...

Writing Things As Ratios

EXAMPLE: Write down the ratio of pink squares to white squares in this pattern.

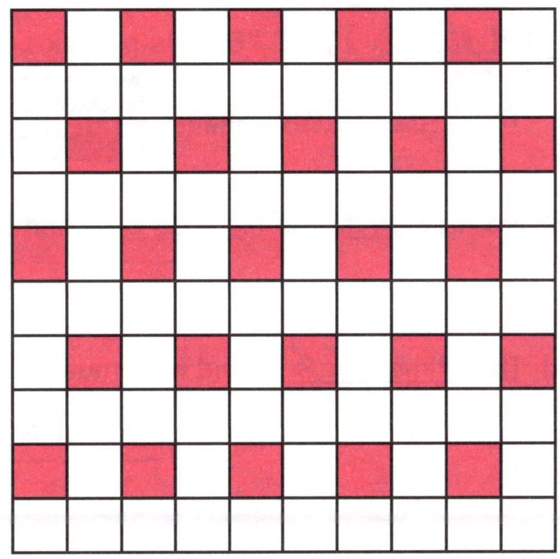

ANSWER:

1) First count the number of pink squares and the number of white squares:
   Pink = 25 White = 75

2) Now write the numbers with the : sign in between:
   Pink:White is 25:75.

3) You might need to simplify this by cancelling down the numbers (see below).

Simplifying Ratios

1) Simplifying ratios is the same as cancelling down fractions (see page 7).

2) Find a number that will go into both bits of the ratio, then divide them both by that number.

3) E.g. for the ratio 25:75 in the example above, 25 will go into both bits of the ratio. So dividing both numbers by 25 gives a simplified ratio of 1:3.

EXAMPLE: Bill is 18 and Ted is 27.
Give the ratio of Bill's age to Ted's age in its simplest form.

ANSWER:

1) The ratio of Bill's age to Ted's age is 18:27.

2) 9 will go into both 18 and 27.

3) 18 ÷ 9 = 2, and 27 ÷ 9 = 3.

4) So the simplified ratio is 2:3.

The order of the numbers is important — make sure you put Bill's age first as it asks in the question.

Ratios

Some exam questions on ratios can be a bit more wordy.
But most of them can be done using the same GOLDEN RULE...

DIVIDE FOR ONE, THEN TIMES FOR ALL

Example 1:

"5 pints of milk cost £1.30. How much will 3 pints cost?"

1) The GOLDEN RULE says: **DIVIDE FOR ONE, THEN TIMES FOR ALL**

2) So first divide the price by 5 to find how much it costs FOR ONE PINT:

£1.30 ÷ 5 = 0.26 = 26p (for 1 pint)

3) Then times by 3 to find how much it costs FOR 3 PINTS:

26p × 3 = 78p (for 3 pints)

Example 2:

"This recipe for Rat and Toad Pie serves 4 people.
Change these amounts so there's enough for SIX."

4 Fresh Rats (frozen will do)
2 Toads
8 Dirty Potatoes
(Plus a big bit of pastry)

1) First DIVIDE each amount by 4 to get enough for ONE PERSON.

2) Then TIMES by 6 to get enough for SIX.

4 Rats ÷ 4 = 1 Rat (for one person) ×6 = 6 Rats (for 6 people)

2 Toads ÷ 4 = 0.5 Toads (for one person) ×6 = 3 Toads (for 6 people)

8 Potatoes ÷ 4 = 2 potatoes (for one person) ×6 = 12 potatoes (for 6 people)

(Plus an even bigger bit of pastry...)

Remember — "divide for one, then times for all"...

It's a simple rule — the trick is knowing when to use it. Learning the examples above will help.

1) If seven pencils cost 70p, how much will 4 pencils cost?
2) Work out the amount of each ingredient needed to make enough Rat and Toad Pie for 9 people.*

*If you could e-mail me your answer, that would be great — I'm holding a dinner party next Saturday.

Revision Test for Unit 1 — 1

1) These are the sort of numbers you might get in your calculator display:
a) 1.2343534 b) 2.9999999 c) 15.534624 d) 12.0833
Round them off to the nearest whole number.

2) a) Round 246 to the nearest 10. b) Round 860 to the nearest 100.

3) Round these numbers off to 1 decimal place: a) 5.32 b) 3.46 c) 6.15

4) Write an equivalent fraction for each of these:
a) $\frac{1}{4}$ b) $\frac{2}{5}$ c) $\frac{7}{6}$

Remember, equivalent means equal in size.

5) What number should go on the top of the fraction $\frac{?}{40}$ to make it equivalent to $\frac{3}{10}$?

Hint: you do the same to the top and bottom.

6) Simplify $\frac{5}{15}$.

7) Cancel down $\frac{25}{100}$ as far as possible so that it's in its simplest form.

8) Calculate: a) $\frac{3}{5}$ of 250 b) $\frac{4}{7}$ of 280

9) Shona buys a sofa costing £600. She pays $\frac{2}{3}$ of the cost straight away and the rest later.
How much does Shona pay straight away?

10) Calculate 35% of 160.

11) Carl puts £300 in the bank. He makes 5% interest on his money.
a) What is 5% of £300? b) How much money does he have in total?

12) What is 8 as a percentage of 160?

13) Write down the ratio of circles to squares.

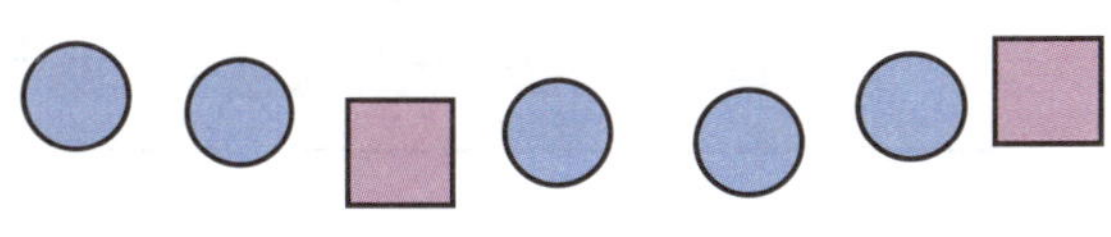

14) Write these ratios in their simplest form.
a) 8:20 b) 65:25 c) 54:81

15) Last week Rick ordered 5 pints of milk from the milkman. He paid £2.35 for the milk.
This week he orders 3 pints of milk. How much will he pay this week?

Types of Data

Data is a fancy word for information. There are different types of data, which also have fancy names...

Data Can Be Primary Or Secondary

PRIMARY data is data YOU'VE collected.

There are two main ways you can get primary data:

- A SURVEY, e.g. a questionnaire.
- An EXPERIMENT (like you do in science lessons).

SECONDARY data is collected by SOMEONE ELSE.

There are lots of ways you can get secondary data, e.g. from:

- newspapers
- the internet
- databases
- historical records

Data can be Qualitative Or Quantitative

Think 'quantity means numbers' as a way to remember which is which.

QUALITATIVE data is in WORD form.

For example:

- gender (male or female)
- eye colour
- favourite football team

QUANTITATIVE data is in NUMBER form.

For example:

- heights of people
- the time taken to do a task
- the weight of objects

Quantitative Data is Discrete or Continuous

DISCRETE DATA can be measured exactly — in whole numbers or certain values.

For example:

- the number of goals scored
- the number of people in a shop
- the number of pages in this book

CONTINUOUS DATA can take any value over a certain range.

For example:

- the height of this page (it's 297 mm to the nearest mm but that's not its exact height)
- the weight of a pumpkin
- the length of a carrot

Sorry, I can't date 'er — she's just not my type...

Just lots of words to learn on this page then. Once you've got that done, try this question:

1) Say whether this data is qualitative, discrete or continuous:

a) The number of people at a rugby match.
b) The colours of pebbles on a beach.
c) The names of people visiting a park on a certain day.
d) The lengths of fish in a pond.

Questionnaires

Questionnaires are a good way of collecting data — they're cheap and easy to give to lots of people.

Design Your Questionnaire Carefully

Most survey questions have a fixed number of answers, e.g. yes/no or tick box questions.
Think about the six points below when you get a question on questionnaires:

QUESTIONNAIRE ABOUT HOBBIES

1) How do you get to school? Please tick:

Bus ☐ Car ☐ Bicycle ☐

Walking ☐ Other ☐

2) What manner of recreational activities do you partake in to while away your leisure time?

....

3) What is your favourite sport?

Football ☐ Hockey ☐

Baseball ☐ Tennis ☐

4) Do you agree that knitting is the best hobby? Yes /

5) Do you play computer games a lot? Yes / No

6) How old are you? ....

1 QUESTIONS SHOULD BE RELEVANT
The question needs to be useful — this one has nothing to do with hobbies so it shouldn't be there.

2 QUESTIONS SHOULD BE CLEAR, SHORT AND EASY TO UNDERSTAND
This one isn't, so change it.

3 ALLOW FOR ALL POSSIBLE ANSWERS
This is hard to answer if you like rugby best.
Add an 'other' box to allow for other answers.

4 QUESTIONS SHOULDN'T BE LEADING
Leading questions are ones that suggest what the answer should be. "What is your favourite hobby?" is a better question here.

5 ANSWERS SHOULD BE CLEAR
It's not clear here what 'a lot' means. "How many hours do you play per week?" is better.

6 PEOPLE MAY NOT TELL THE TRUTH
They might be embarrassed about the answer. Here it'd be better to give an age group to choose from instead.

Who wants to collect a questionnaire...

... is the (not so exciting) quiz spin-off. Make sure you learn this page and then try this question...

1) Give one thing that's wrong with each of these questions: a) Do you watch a lot of television?
b) Do you agree that maths is the most important school subject?
c) What is your favourite drink? Answer A, B or C. A) Tea B) Milk C) Coffee

Collecting Data

If you're doing a survey or experiment, you'll need an observation sheet to record your results.

Observation Sheets Need Enough Space

1) An observation sheet is just a big table that you can fill in with results as you collect them.

2) It needs to have enough space for all the data you want to write down.

3) It should be set out in a way that makes it as easy as possible for you to collect data:

EXAMPLE 1:
Dave is asking 20 people in his class how much they spend on food and drink at lunchtime.
He needs enough space to write down how much 20 people spend on both food and drink.
He needs a table like this, but with 20 rows.

Student	Food (£)	Drink (£)	Total (£)
1	2.52	0.95	3.47
2			
3			

Put a mark here for every time you get 'heads'. Then add them up.

Heads	Tails
~~IIII~~ I	IIII
6	4

EXAMPLE 2:
You could use a simple tally chart to collect data on coin tossing.

Split Data Into Groups Called Classes

1) If there's a lot of data, or if it's very spread out, it's better to group it into different classes.

2) Choose the classes carefully so none of them overlap.
Make sure each bit of data can only be put into one class.

3) For example, if you were collecting data on ages, it makes more sense to have age groups as shown below, instead of saying how many people were 15, how many were 16, etc.

Age in full years	0 – 19	20 – 39	40 – 59	60 – 79	80 – 99
Number of people	6	13	14	8	9

4) The problem with grouping data is that it's less accurate because you don't have the individual values any more. E.g. you can't tell how many people are exactly 20 years old.

"You said Clowns... and our survey said... 43... that's a top answer..."

If you learn this stuff properly, then maybe one day you too could work for a top game show...

Sampling

There's so much data out there that we take samples to make things simpler.

Sampling — Cheaper and Easier than Asking Everyone

1) We usually collect information about a group of people or things. This whole group is called a POPULATION.

   E.g. if you want to know the heights of people in your school, then the population is everyone in the school.

2) You can collect data by doing a SURVEY of either the population or a SAMPLE. A sample is just a PART OF THE POPULATION.

3) The sample has to represent the population fairly — this means that the overall results from the sample should be more or less the same as if they'd come from the whole population.

4) To make sure the sample represents the population fairly, it has to be big enough, chosen at random, and there must be the right mix of boys/girls, ages, etc. to match the whole group.

If it doesn't represent the population fairly, it's a biased sample.

There are pros and cons of using samples:

PROS	CONS
It's a lot quicker, cheaper and often easier than asking the whole group.	You don't have results from everyone in the population so it can be less accurate.

Spotting Biased Samples

To make sure you can spot an unfair or biased sample, here's a lovely example:

EXAMPLE: In a telephone survey, 100 people in a town were asked if they often use trains. 20% said yes. Does this mean 20% of the people in the country often go by train?

ANSWER: Probably not. This could be a biased sample because:

1) The sample is too small. At least 1000 people would be better.
2) People who don't have a phone won't be included.
3) The time of day people were phoned might make it biased. E.g. in the daytime, people who take the train to work would be out.
4) People from all over the country should have been called, not just one town — if there's no station in the town then people there might not use trains as much.
5) People should have been sampled at random (it doesn't say they weren't but make sure).

When getting a sample — size matters...

...so that it's fair. Have a go at this question: 1) A survey about what type of music people in a school like uses one Year 7 class as a sample. Could this be a biased sample? Explain why / why not.

Mode, Median, Mean and Range

If you learn the 3 types of average (the mode, median and mean) — and what the range is — then you'll be well set for some juicy exam marks. But there's one thing you must remember...

THE GOLDEN RULE:

Always WRITE THE NUMBERS in SIZE ORDER first

E.g. If you had a list of shoe sizes like this: 6, 7, 5, 5, 4, 9, 3
you'd need to write out the list again in SIZE ORDER, like this: 3, 4, 5, 5, 6, 7, 9

We usually go from smallest to biggest.

There Are Three Types of Average

1) MODE = MOST common

Mode = most (think of the 'o' when you say them)

2) MEDIAN = MIDDLE value

Median = mid (think of the m*d when you say them)

EXAMPLE:

In the list of shoe sizes:

3, 4, 5, 5, 6, 7, 9

The mode is '5' because it's the most common (it appears the most in the list).

The median is also '5' because it's the middle number.

3) MEAN = TOTAL of items ÷ NUMBER of items

Mean is what most people think of when they say the average.
It's mean because you have to do a calculation to work it out.

You'll see how to do this on the next page.

Range is How Spread Out Things Are

RANGE = Biggest Number − Smallest Number

The range is NOT a type of average.
It's useful for seeing how spread out things are.
For example, in the list of shoe sizes above,
the biggest shoe size is 9 and the smallest is 3.
So the range of shoe sizes = 9 − 3 = 6.

Don't forget the order — socks and then shoes...

Learn the four blue boxes and the Golden Rule, then cover this page and write them all down.
Then you're ready for the next page — bet you can't wait...

Mode, Median, Mean and Range

Think you've got the last page sorted? Good. Let's have a look at another example then...

Example:

Find the MODE, MEDIAN, MEAN and RANGE of these numbers:

2, 5, 3, 2, 6, -4, 0, 9, -3, 1, 6, 3, -2, 3

There are 14 numbers in the list so make a note of this.

FIRST... the GOLDEN RULE:
Write the numbers in size order: -4, -3, -2, 0, 1, 2, 2, 3, 3, 3, 5, 6, 6, 9 (✓14)

Mode:

MODE = most common value, which is simply 3.
This is because the number '3' appears most in the list.
(You can also say "The modal value is 3")

This bear is NOT smarter than the average bear.

Median:

MEDIAN = the middle value when they're arranged in order of size.

-4, -3, -2, 0, 1, 2, 2, 3, 3, 3, 5, 6, 6, 9
← seven numbers this side ↑ seven numbers this side →

When there are two middle numbers, as in this case, then the median is halfway between the two middle numbers.

To find the halfway point, add them together and divide by 2: Median = (2 + 3) ÷ 2 = 2.5

Mean:

To find the MEAN — add up all the numbers in the list and divide by how many there are.

$$\text{MEAN} = \frac{\text{total}}{\text{number}} = \frac{-4-3-2+0+1+2+2+3+3+3+5+6+6+9}{14}$$

$$= 31 \div 14 = 2.21$$

Range:

RANGE = distance from lowest to highest value, i.e. from -4 up to 9 = 13.

I don't mean to be mean — this stuff's important...

1) Use what you've learnt on the last 2 pages to find the mean, median, mode and range for this list:
1, 3, 14, -5, 6, -12, 18, 7, 23, 10, -5, -14, 0, 25, 8

Frequency Tables

Frequency tables are like tally charts (see p.16). They can either be done in rows or in columns of numbers. They're not too bad if you learn these key points:

1) The word FREQUENCY means HOW MANY.
So a frequency table is just a 'How many in each group' table.

2) The FIRST ROW (or column) gives the GROUP LABELS.

3) The FREQUENCY ROW (or column) tells you HOW MANY THERE ARE in that group.

You can use frequency tables to help draw things like bar charts (p.25) and pie charts (p.26-27).

Example:

46 pupils in a school were asked how many sisters they had.
The results were put into a frequency table as shown:

In Rows:

Group labels.

No. of Sisters	0	1	2	3	4	5	6	Total:
Tally	卌 ||	卌 卌 卌	卌 卌 ||	卌 |||	|||	|		
Frequency	7	15	12	8	3	1	0	46

The tally column is usually left out.

The frequency is just a total of the tally for that group.

In Columns:

No. of Sisters	Frequency
0	7
1	15
2	12
3	8
4	3
5	1
6	0
Total:	46

You can use the table to find the averages and range:

1) The MODE is the group with the HIGHEST FREQUENCY.

In this case most people asked said they had 1 sister, so the MODE is 1.

2) The table tells us there are people with anything from '0 sisters' right up to '5 sisters' (but NOT 6 sisters).

So the RANGE is 5 – 0 = 5.

3) To find the MEAN you need to add an extra row to the table — see next page.

My table has 5 columns, 6 rows and 4 legs...

The best way of getting your head round this stuff is to practise doing it, so have a go yourself. You could ask your class how many times they've been to London, then put the results in a frequency table.

Finding The Mean from Frequency Tables

So you're feeling okay with frequency tables now? Good. One last thing to learn then. Finding the mean may seem hard at first, but take your time and learn the steps...

You Need To Add An Extra Row

Let's look again at our frequency table of sisters from the last page:

No. of Sisters	0	1	2	3	4	5	6	Total:
Frequency	7	15	12	8	3	1	0	46

(People asked)

1) If we had a list of the number of sisters everyone had, it would look like this:
0, 0, 0, 0, 0, 0, 0, 1, 1, 1, 1, 1, 1, 1, 1, 1, 1, 1, 1, 1, 1, 1, 2, 2, 2, 2, 2, 2, 2, 2....
7 lots of 0 — 15 lots of 1

2) There would be 46 numbers in the list because that's how many people were asked.

3) To find the mean from the list you would have to add up all the numbers and divide by 46.

4) It's exactly the same for the table — except we cheat by adding an extra row:

No. of Sisters	0	1	2	3	4	5	6	Total:
Frequency	7	15	12	8	3	1	0	46
No. × Frequency	0 × 7 = 0	1 × 15 = 15	2 × 12 = 24	3 × 8 = 24	4 × 3 = 12	5 × 1 = 5	6 × 0 = 0	0 + 15 + 24 + 24 + 12 + 5 + 0 = 80

This is the same as adding 7 lots of 0.

This is the same as adding 3 lots of 4.

This is the same as adding up all the numbers in the list. It's the total number of sisters.

5) Now from the table:

MEAN = 3rd Row Total ÷ 2nd Row Total
= 80 ÷ 46 = 1.74 (sisters per person)

Mean sisters

Always Follow These Steps...

1) Add up the TOTAL of the SECOND ROW (or column).
2) Make a THIRD ROW (or column) by MULTIPLYING the FIRST ROW and SECOND ROW together.
3) Add up the TOTAL of the new THIRD ROW.
4) MEAN = 3rd Row total ÷ 2nd Row Total

Do you know what I mean...?

I'm not going to lie and say that was an easy page, but it's really not as bad as it looks. The trick is to learn the 4 steps in the red box and do it every time you're asked for the mean from a table.

Line Graphs and Pictograms

Data can be shown in different types of charts, tables and graphs. Line graphs and pictograms make it easier to see what the data shows than if it was just written in a list or a table.

Line Graphs

1) A line graph is a set of points joined with straight lines.
2) They often have 'time' along the bottom to show how something is changing over time:
3) You can draw two line graphs on the same grid to compare the two, as shown below.

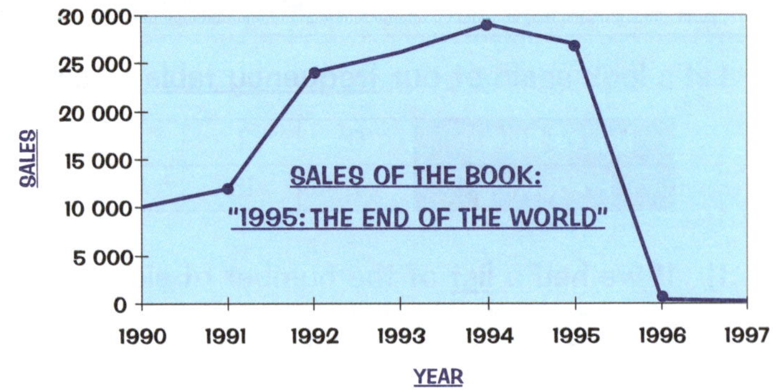

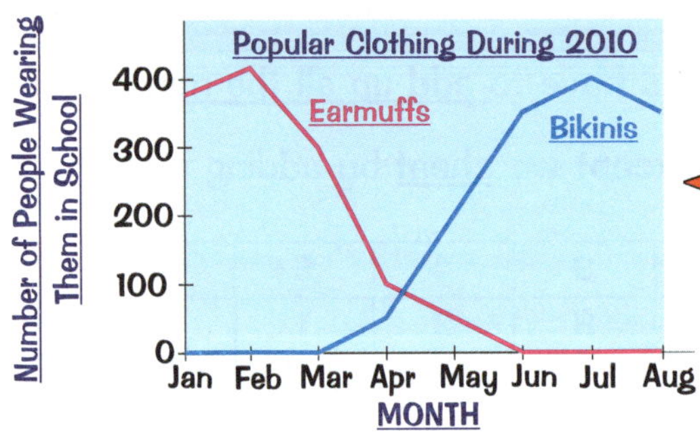

These graphs show clearly that as the year went on, fewer people wore earmuffs and more people wore bikinis...

Pictograms

1) PICTOGRAMS use pictures in place of numbers to show frequency.
2) In a pictogram each picture or symbol represents a certain number of items.

EXAMPLE:

The pictogram below shows the number of talking cats used in TV adverts over 3 months:

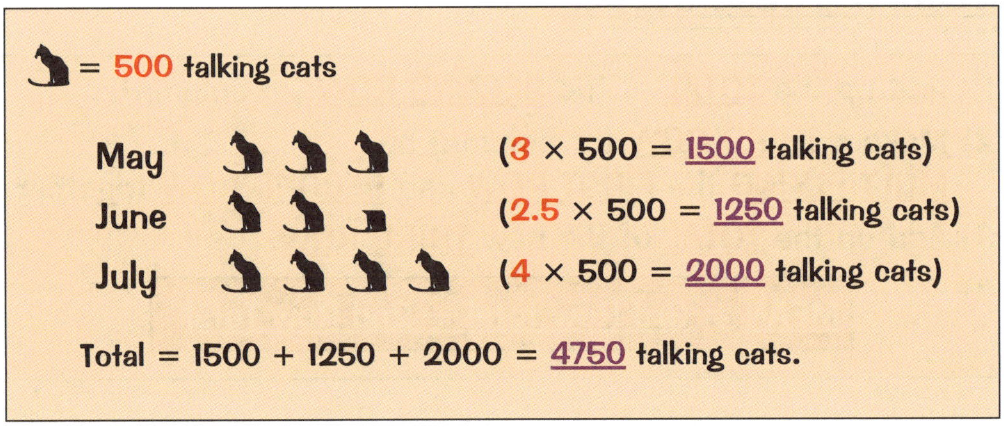

A picture paints a thousand words...

= learn the page, cover it up, and see what you can remember. ...

Two-Way Tables

Two-way tables are a bit like frequency tables but they show two different things at the same time. Like eye colour and hair colour. Or your favourite type of jelly and whether you like mushrooms...

Example:

"Use this table to work out how many

(a) right-handed people and

(b) left-handed women

there were in this survey."

This means that 27 out of the 400 people asked were left-handed men.

	Women	Men	TOTAL
Left-handed		27	63
Right-handed	164	173	
TOTAL	200	200	400

Total left-handed + Total right-handed = Total no. of people

Total no. of women + Total no. of men = Total no. of people

Answer:

(a) To find the number of right-handed people, EITHER:

(i) Add up the number of right-handed women and the number of right-handed men.
So that's 164 + 173 = 337 right-handed people.

OR:

(ii) Take away the total number of left-handed people from the total number of people.
So that's 400 – 63 = 337 right-handed people.

	Women	Men	TOTAL
Left-handed		27	63
Right-handed	164	173	
TOTAL	200	200	400

(b) To find the number of left-handed women, EITHER:

(i) Take away the number of right-handed women from the total number of women.
That's 200 – 164 = 36 left-handed women.

OR:

(ii) Take away the left-handed men from the total number of left-handed people.
Which would be 63 – 27 = 36 left-handed women.

	Women	Men	TOTAL
Left-handed		27	63
Right-handed	164	173	
TOTAL	200	200	400

There's no two ways about it — you've got to learn it...

Try filling out a similar table for the people in your class. Count how many girls are left- or right-handed, and the same for the boys, and add up the totals of the rows and columns. Fun times.

Scatter Graphs

Scatter Graphs Can Show Correlation

1) A SCATTER GRAPH is used to show how two things are related (linked).

2) If they're closely related then the points will lie fairly close to a straight line, called a LINE OF BEST FIT.
You say the data has STRONG CORRELATION.

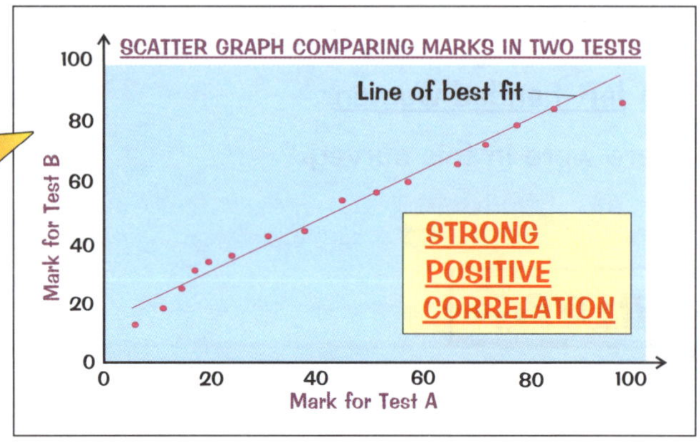

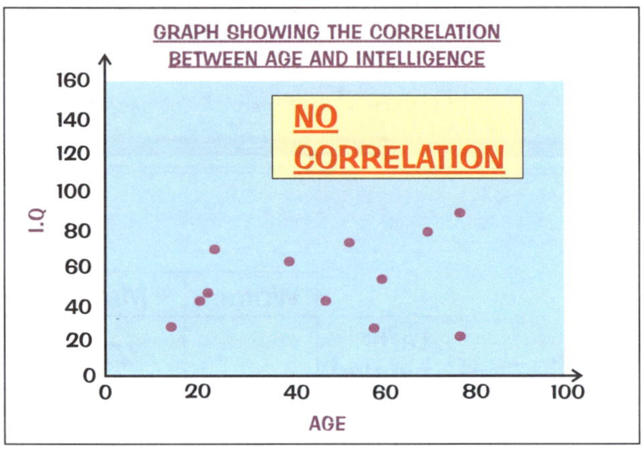

3) If they're not related, you get a load of messy points. You say the data has NO CORRELATION.

4) If the points form a line sloping UPHILL from left to right (like the first graph above), then there is POSITIVE CORRELATION — both things increase or decrease together.

5) If the points form a line sloping DOWNHILL from left to right (like the graph below), then there is NEGATIVE CORRELATION — as one thing increases the other decreases.

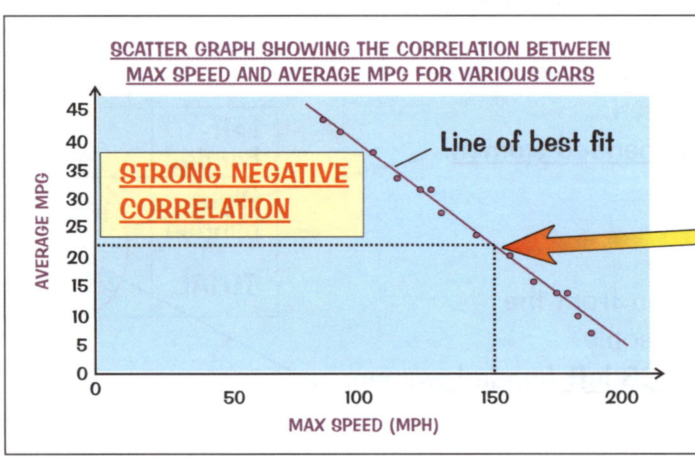

You can use the line of best fit to predict other values. E.g. you would expect a car with a max speed of 150 mph to average 22 mpg.

What soap do maths teachers watch — Correlation Street...

There is a strong positive correlation between evil laughing/cat stroking/beard combing and how much of an evil genius you are. Learn this page and try drawing an example of each type of scatter graph.

Bar Charts

Bar Charts Show Data As Bars

1) The height of each bar is the frequency for that group.

2) Watch out for when the bars should touch or not touch:

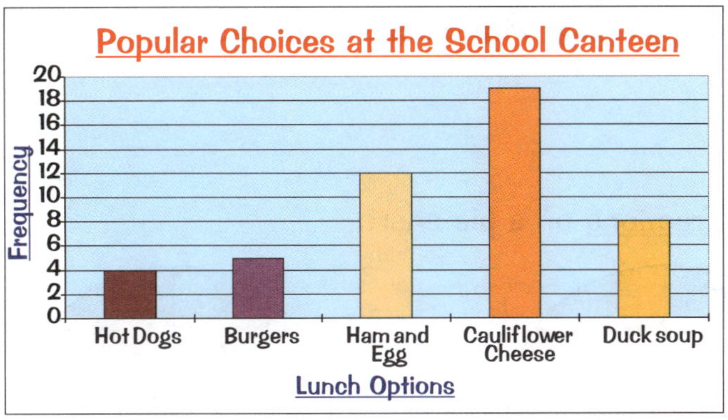

This bar chart compares separate items (e.g. hot dogs, burgers) so the bars don't touch.

A bar-line graph is just like a bar chart except you draw thin lines instead of bars.

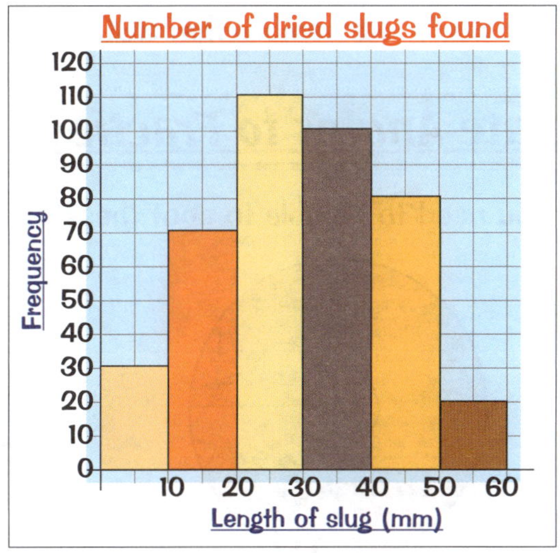

ALL the bars in this chart are for LENGTHS — every possible length must be included so there should be no spaces between the bars.

Dual Bar Charts Can be Used to Compare Things

1) Dual bar charts show two sets of data together so you can compare them.

2) Each category has two bars — one for each set of data.

3) The dual bar chart on the right shows the favourite colours of a group of pupils, but it's split into two sets — boys and girls.

4) The bar chart shows, for example, that green was the most popular colour for girls, but red was the favourite for boys.

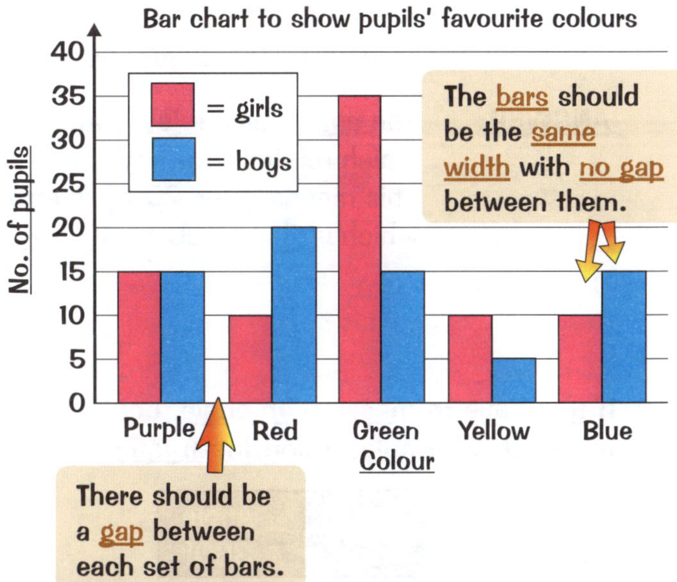

A sheep's favourite graph — the baaaa chart...

Woah, have another read of this page, then test yourself with this lovely question.

1) Use this table to draw a dual bar chart showing how the four teams scored in each round of a quiz.

Hint: Each colour team should have two bars — one for each round.

Team Name	Green	Blue	Red	Yellow
Points — 1st round	24	15	20	25
Points — 2nd round	16	15	22	20

Pie Charts

Just as you can make a yummy pie from the right mix of meat and pastry, examiners can make meaty exam questions from pie charts. So learn the GOLDEN RULE for pie charts:

The TOTAL of Everything = 360°

Remember that 360° is the trick for dealing with most pie charts.

Relate Angles to Fractions

1) You need to be able to spot these common fractions on a pie chart:

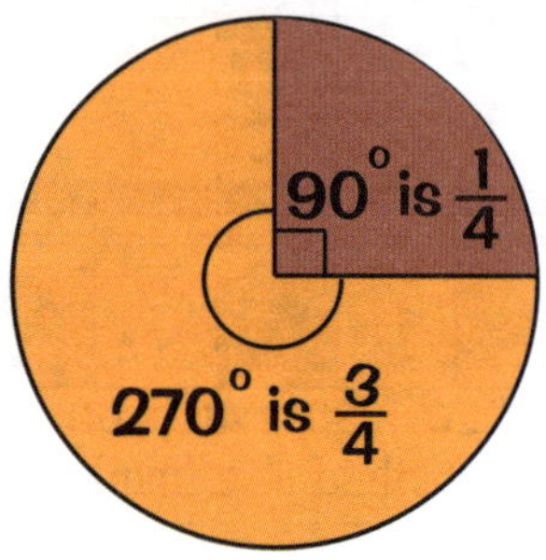

90° is $\frac{1}{4}$
270° is $\frac{3}{4}$

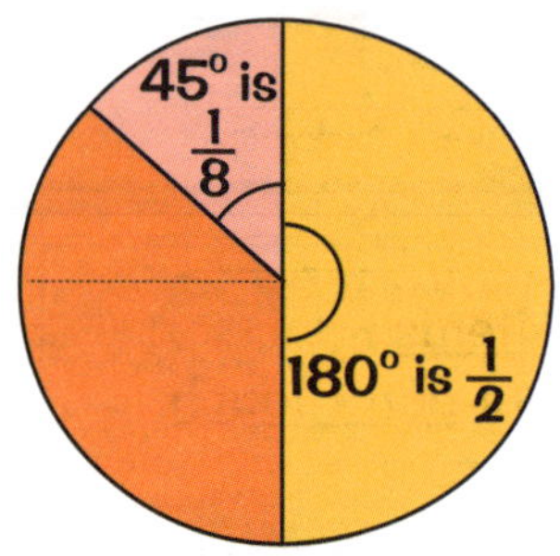

45° is $\frac{1}{8}$
180° is $\frac{1}{2}$

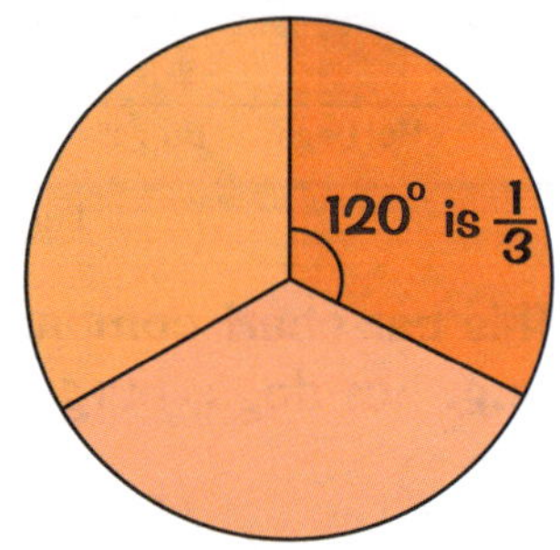

120° is $\frac{1}{3}$

EXAMPLE: A group of 200 people were asked to choose their favourite type of cat. The results are shown in this pie chart. How many people prefer evil cats?

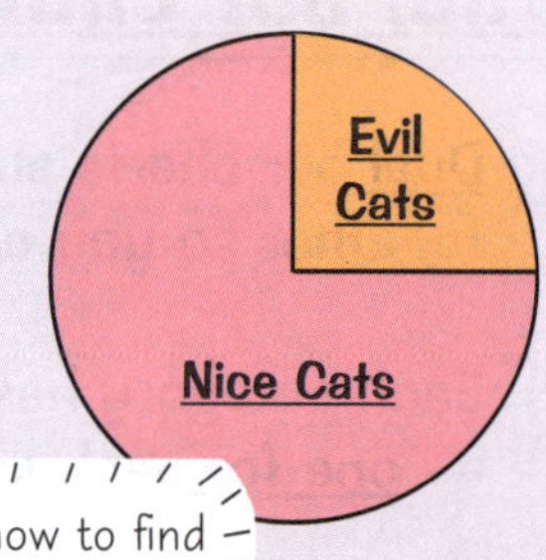

ANSWER: The angle for the 'evil cats' group is 90°, which relates to a fraction of $\frac{1}{4}$.
This means $\frac{1}{4}$ of 200 preferred evil cats, which is $\frac{1}{4} \times 200 = 50$ people.

See page 7 for how to find fractions of amounts.

2) If you have to measure an angle, you'll need to use this formula to find the fraction:

$$\text{Fraction} = \frac{\text{Angle}}{360°}$$

Have a look at page 93 if you're not sure how to measure an angle.

3) For example, if the angle for a group is 36°, the fraction is $36 \div 360 = \frac{1}{10}$.
So the number of things in that group will be $\frac{1}{10}$ of the total.

Pie Charts

Work Out Angles to Draw Pie Charts

EXAMPLE: The table below shows the results of a survey on the animals people are most afraid of. Draw a pie chart to show these results.

Creature	Hamsters	Guinea pigs	Rabbits	Ducks	Stick insects	Total
Number	20	17	15	26	12	90 ← ①
	③ ↓ ×4	↓	↓	↓	↓	↓ ×4 ← ②
Angle	80°					360°

1) Add up all the numbers in each sector to get the TOTAL (=90).

2) Then find the number that you need to times the total by to get 360°. 360 ÷ 90 = 4, so the total needs to be multiplied by 4 to make 360°.

3) Now MULTIPLY EVERY NUMBER BY 4 to get the angle for each group. E.g. the angle for hamsters is 20 × 4 = 80°.

4) Draw a 'start line' somewhere in the circle and draw the angle of one group from this line. Use this angle line as the start line for the next angle, and carry on until all the angles are done.

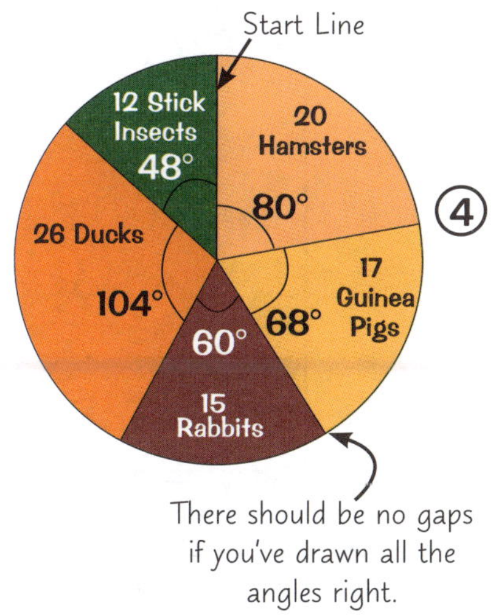

Use the Total to Find the Other Numbers

EXAMPLE: In the pie chart on the right, there are 9 pets in total. How many dogs are there?

ANSWER:

1) Divide 360° by the total number of pets: 360° ÷ 9 = 40°. 40° represents one pet.

2) Divide each of the angles given by 40° to get the number of pets for those groups. So there are 2 cats and 3 mice, as shown.

3) The final bit of pie is what's left over: 9 – 2 – 3 = 4 pet dogs.

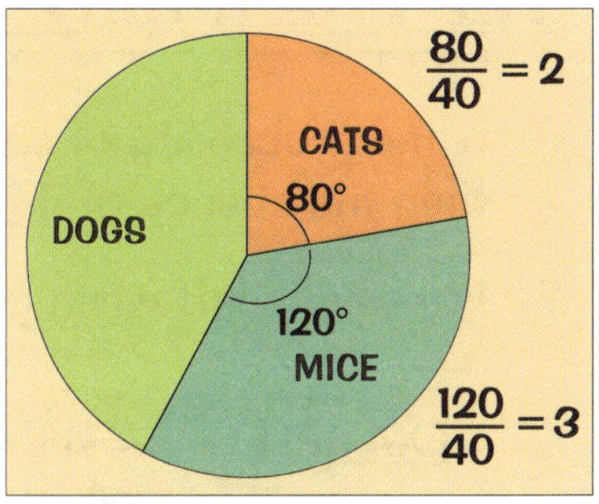

I bet you were expecting a joke about pies here...

... I'm far too witty to bother making jokes about pies on a page about pie charts. There's just no need to go on about tasty steak-filled pies on a bed of creamy mash and a side order of mushy peas... mmm.

1) Anyway, while I'm off eating pies, you can draw a pie chart for this table:

Football Team	Wigan A.	Luton	Man Utd	Others
No. of fans	53	15	30	22

Probability

The probability of something happening (an 'event') is how likely it is to happen.
Probability is given a number, so we can do loads of lovely maths with it. Hurrah.

All Probabilities Are Between 0 and 1

1) Probabilities can only have values from 0 to 1 (including 0 and 1).

2) You should be able to put the probability of any event happening on this scale of 0 to 1.

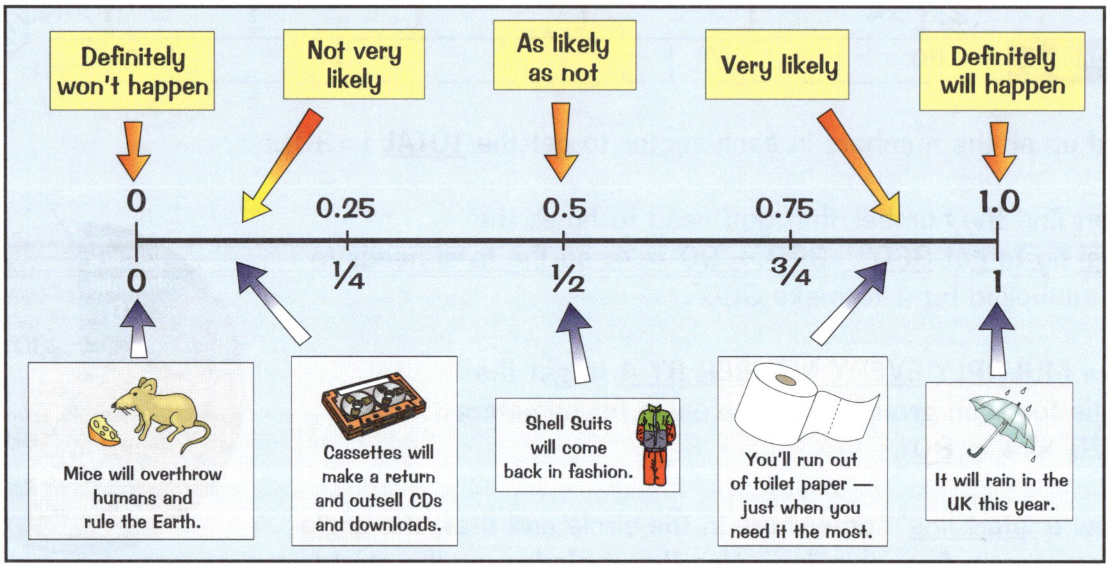

3) You can give probabilities using FRACTIONS, DECIMALS or PERCENTAGES.
E.g. a probability of ½ can also be written as 0.5 or 50%.

4) To save on words, we can write e.g:
'the probability of tossing a coin and getting a head is 0.5' as: P(H) = 0.5.

P is for probability

H is for head

The Probability Of Something Not Happening = 1 – P

1) If the probability of something happening is 0.3,
then the chance of it NOT HAPPENING is 1 – 0.3 = 0.7.

2) It's what's left when you subtract it from 1 (or 100% for percentages).

EXAMPLE: A spinner has a 0.25 chance of landing on TWO.
What's the probability of it NOT landing on two?

ANSWER: P(2) = 0.25, so P(not 2) = 1 – 0.25 = 0.75.
So, the chance of the spinner not landing on two is 0.75.

P(2) means the probability of getting a 2.

This is probably my favourite topic...

It's very likely that you'll get a question on probability in the exam, so learn this page and answer these:
1) The probability of the local roller derby team winning a match is ¾.
a) Are they likely or unlikely to win? b) What is the probability of them NOT winning?

Equal and Unequal Probabilities

It's all fun and games on this page. And a bit of maths. Oh yes.

Equal Probabilities

1) When the different results or 'outcomes' of something happening all have the same chance of happening, then the probabilities will be EQUAL.

2) These are the two cases which usually come up in exams:

1) TOSSING A COIN:	Equal chance of getting a head or a tail (probability $= \frac{1}{2}$)
2) THROWING A DICE:	Equal chance of getting any of the numbers (probability $= \frac{1}{6}$)

3) Notice that the probability depends on the number of possible outcomes. E.g. there are 6 different ways a dice can land, so the probability of any one of them is '1 out of 6' or $\frac{1}{6}$.

Unequal Probabilities

In most cases, different outcomes have different probabilities — some are more likely than others.

EXAMPLE 1: "A bag contains 6 blue balls, 5 red balls and 9 green balls. Find P(green)."

ANSWER: The chances of picking out the three colours are NOT EQUAL because there are different numbers of balls in each colour. The probability of picking a green is:

$$P(\text{green}) = \frac{\text{NUMBER OF GREENS}}{\text{TOTAL NUMBER OF BALLS}} = \frac{9}{20}$$

EXAMPLE 2: "What is the probability of winning £45 on this spinner?"

ANSWER:
The pointer has the same chance of stopping on every sector.
There are 2 out of 8 which say £45, so:

$P(£45) = \frac{2}{8} = \frac{1}{4}$ (as a fraction)
or 0.25 (as a decimal)
or 25% (as a percentage)

See page 45 for how to swap between fractions, decimals and percentages.

It's enough to make your head spin...

Spinners and bags of balls come up a lot in the exam. Don't panic if they use another example — you work it out in exactly the same way. Try this one: 1) What is the probability of picking a white puppy from a bag containing 3 black puppies, 4 brown puppies, 2 white puppies and 1 purple puppy?

Listing Outcomes

The key to working out probabilities is finding the number of outcomes.
But sometimes it's not clear straight away just how many different outcomes there are.

Listing All Outcomes: Use a Sample Space

1) You might get asked to list all the possible outcomes for TWO THINGS HAPPENING TOGETHER. A simple question might be to list all the possible results from tossing two coins:

Here H is for heads and T is for tails.

The possible outcomes from TOSSING TWO COINS are:

HH HT TH TT

'TT' just means both coins show tails.

2) You can work out probabilities from your list. E.g. P(TT) = $\frac{1}{4}$, because there are 4 outcomes in total, and only 1 of these is TT.

3) For harder questions, you're better off listing all the possible results in a sample space diagram — a posh name for a table.

4) The sample space for spinning these two spinners is shown below:

	Red	Blue	Green
1	1R	1B	1G
2	2R	2B	2G
3	3R	3B	3G

3 different outcomes on colour spinner.

3 different outcomes on number spinner.

5) Any number on the number spinner could come up with any colour on the colour spinner. Spinning them together gives $3 \times 3 = 9$ different combinations altogether. The sample space is a list of these 9 outcomes.

6) The probability of spinning e.g. a 2 and a GREEN (2G) is 1 out of 9, so **P(2G) = $\frac{1}{9}$.**

7) If both spinners are number spinners, you can also fill in the sample space with the total of the two numbers:

	1	2	3
1	2	3	4
2	3	4	5
3	4	5	6

3 different outcomes on 2nd number spinner.

3 different outcomes on 1st number spinner.

These are the totals of the two spinners, e.g. 3 + 3 = 6.

Understanding probability — the outcome of learning this page...

A sample space is a really handy way of making sure you've not missed out any possible outcomes.
1) Draw a sample space for rolling two dice together (both numbered 1-6), and answer these questions:
a) How many outcomes are there in total? b) How many of the outcomes result in a total of 8?
c) What is the probability of rolling a total of 8 on the dice, P(8)?

Revision Test for Unit 1 — 2

1) Gerald is collecting data for himself about shoe sizes of people in his school. Is this data:
a) primary or secondary? b) qualitative or quantitative? c) discrete or continuous?

2) In his survey, Gerald asks the question: "Do you have big feet?".
Give two things that are wrong with this question.

3) Gerald thinks he will have too much information if he writes down the shoe size of every person in the school. Suggest two things that would make it easier to collect the data.

4) For this set of numbers:
2, 6, 7, 12, 3, 7, 4, 15
a) Find the MODE b) Find the MEDIAN
c) Find the MEAN d) Find the RANGE

5) What is this type of diagram called?
How many angry customers were there on Thursday?

6) A newspaper says that the scatter graph shown here shows a strong positive correlation between eating cheese and having nightmares.
Do you agree with the newspaper?

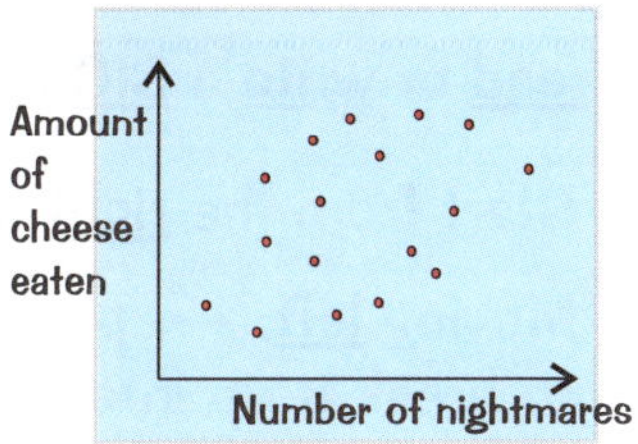

7) Fiona has done a traffic survey for her Geography coursework.
She wants to show the information in a pie chart.
a) Complete Fiona's table.
b) Draw the PIE CHART.

Car Colour	Blue	Red	Yellow	White	Totals:
Number of Cars	12	15	4	9	40
Angle on Pie Chart					360°

8) The probability of rolling SIX on a biased dice is 0.2.
What is the chance of NOT rolling a six?

A biased dice has a higher chance of landing on some numbers than others.

9) Colin has made a game for the summer fair. In a bag he has 3 red balls, 5 green balls and 7 black balls. If you pick a red ball you win a prize.
What is the probability of winning Colin's game, as a percentage?

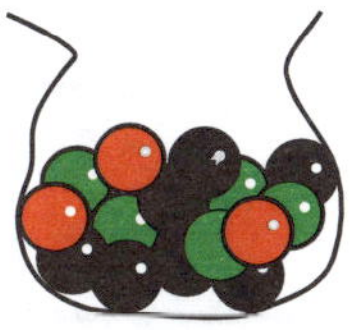

10) I toss a coin and throw a dice at the same time.
a) List all the possible outcomes in a sample space.
b) What is the probability of getting a HEAD and a SIX?

Ordering Numbers

Here's a cracking page to get you started on Unit 2. You need to be able to:
1) Read big numbers 2) Write them down 3) Put them in order of size.

Split Big Numbers Into Columns and Parts

1) First, you really need to know the names of all the columns. E.g. for the number 2 351 243:

2	3	5	1	2	4	3
MILLIONS	HUNDRED-THOUSANDS	TEN-THOUSANDS	THOUSANDS	HUNDREDS	TENS	UNITS

These are the names of the columns.

2) You can then split any number up into its parts, like this:

2 000 000	Two million
300 000	Three hundred thousand
50 000	Fifty thousand
1 000	One thousand
200	Two hundred
40	Four tens (forty)
3	Three units

→ These add together to make 2 351 243 again.

Line up the columns so you can read the numbers clearly.

Look at Big Numbers in Groups of Three

To read or write a BIG number, follow these steps:

1) Start from the right-hand side of the number →
2) Moving left, ←, put a space every 3 digits to break it up into groups of 3.
3) Now going right, →, read each group of three as a separate number, as shown.

2 351 243

MILLIONS THOUSANDS The rest

So read as: 2 million, 351 thousand, 243
or write fully in words:
Two million, three hundred and fifty-one thousand, two hundred and forty-three.

Putting Numbers in Order of Size

EXAMPLE: Put the following in order from smallest to biggest:

623 32 486 4563 75 4143

① First put them into groups, the ones with fewest digits first:

SMALLER	32, 75	623, 486	4563, 4143	BIGGER
	all the 2-digit ones	all the 3-digit ones	all the 4-digit ones	

A digit is a number 0-9 which sits in a column of a bigger number. E.g. in 623, the digits are 6, 2 and 3.

② Then put each group in order of size by comparing the columns left to right:

3 is smaller than 7. — 32, 75

4 is smaller than 6. — 486, 623

The 1st digits are the same so look at the 2nd ones — 1 is smaller than 5. — 4143, 4563

ANSWER: 32 75 486 623 4143 4563

Ordering Numbers

You also need to be able to put decimal numbers in order too. Again, it's all about the columns. After the decimal point the columns are called decimal places.

Split Decimals Into Decimal Places

1) The decimal places have names too. E.g. for the number 41.602:

4 1 . 6 0 2

4 — TENS
1 — UNITS
. — DECIMAL POINT
6 — TENTHS
0 — HUNDREDTHS
2 — THOUSANDTHS

2) You can split up decimals into parts too:

40.000	Four tens (forty)
1.000	One unit
0.600	Six tenths
0.000	Zero hundredths
0.002	Two thousandths

These add together to make 41.602 again.

With decimals, line up the decimal points.

You would read this as forty one point six oh two.

Putting Decimals in Order of Size

EXAMPLE: Put the following in order from smallest to biggest:

2.4 0.004 0.0024 0.024 0.04 0.24 4

① For decimals, do the whole-number bit first before looking at the decimal bit. The numbers 2.4 and 4 have whole numbers, so these must be bigger than the rest.

② Now group the numbers that are left by the number of 0s STRAIGHT AFTER THE POINT. The group with the most 0s comes first, just like this:

SMALLER	two 0s	one 0	no 0s	BIGGER
	0.004 0.0024	0.024 0.04	0.24	

③ Once they're in groups, order them by comparing the decimal places left to right.

2 is smaller than 4. — 0.0024, 0.004

2 is smaller than 4. — 0.024, 0.04

0.24

Don't forget to put your bigger numbers back in the list.

ANSWER: 0.0024 0.004 0.024 0.04 0.24 2.4 4

Don't call numbers big or small to their face — it's rude...

Putting numbers into order of size isn't too tricky — if you learn the tips on the last two pages.

1) Write these numbers in words: a) 1 234 531 b) 23 456 c) 2415 d) 3402 e) 203 412
2) Write this down as a number: Fifty-six thousand, four hundred and twenty-one
3) Put these numbers in order of size (smallest to biggest): 23 493 87 1029 3004 345 9
4) Put these decimals in order of size (smallest to biggest): 0.37 0.008 0.307 0.1 0.09 0.2

Addition and Subtraction

You're not allowed a calculator in your Unit 2 exam, so you need to know how to do sums with just a pen and paper.

Adding

E.g. Add together 292, 484 and 29

1) Line up the units columns of each number.

2) Add up the columns from right to left starting with the units: 2 + 4 + 9 = 15.

   Write the '5' at the bottom of the units column and carry over the '1' to the next column along.

3) Add up the next column, including anything carried over: 9 + 8 + 2 + 1 = 20.
   So put '0' at the bottom and carry over the '2'.

4) Do the same for the last column: 2 + 4 + 2 = 8.

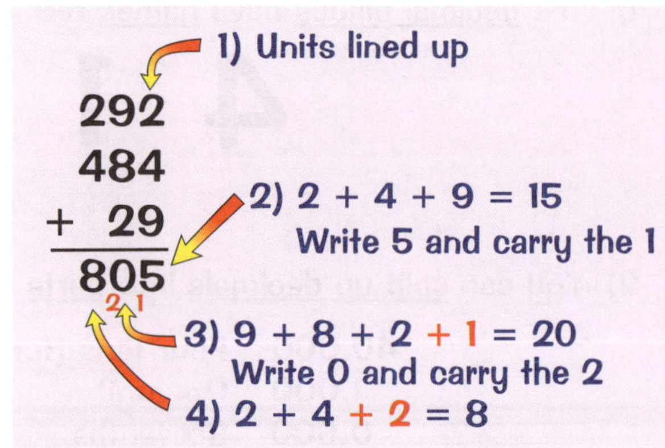

So 292 + 484 + 29 = 805.

Subtracting

E.g. Work out 693 – 665

1) Line up the units columns of each number.

2) Going right to left, take the bottom number away from the top number.

   Here the top number (3) is smaller than the bottom number (5), so borrow 10 from the next column along. The '9' in the tens column becomes '8'.

3) You now have 3 + 10 = 13 units, so you can do the subtraction 13 – 5 = 8. Write the 8 at the bottom.

4) Subtracting the numbers in the next column along gives 8 – 6 = 2, so write 2 at the bottom.

5) In the last column, 6 – 6 = 0.

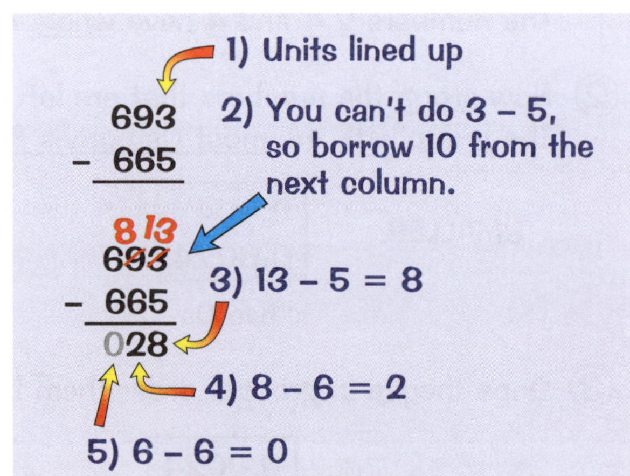

So 693 – 665 = 28.

Who needs a calculator when you have a pen and paper...

Test your skills of pen-and-paper maths with these teasers:

1) Work out: a) 56 + 738 + 12, b) 459 – 273.
2) When Ric was 10 he was 142 cm tall. Since then he has grown 29 cm.
   a) How tall is he now? b) How much taller must he be to be 190 cm tall?

Don't forget to include the units in your answers.

Adding and Subtracting Decimals

The methods for adding and subtracting decimals are just the same as the ones on the last page, but always make sure you LINE UP THE DECIMAL POINTS.

Adding Decimals...

E.g. Work out 3.74 + 24.2 + 0.6

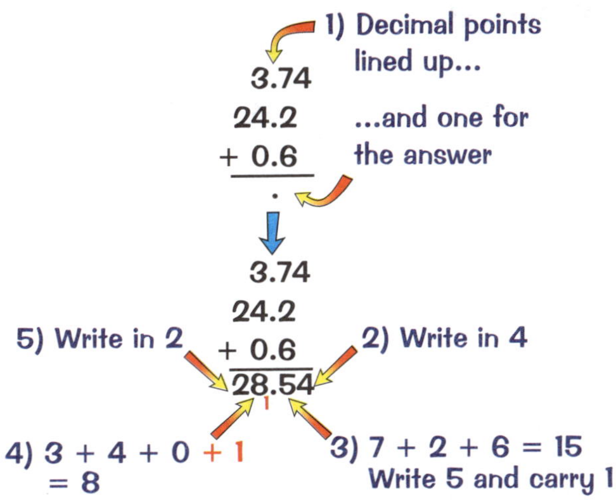

1) LINE UP THE DECIMAL POINTS of each number, making sure all the other columns line up. Put a decimal point in the space for the answer too.
2) Add up the columns from right to left. The first column only has a 4 in it, so write 4 at the bottom of the column.
3) Add up the numbers in the next column along: 7 + 2 + 6 = 15. Write the '5' at the bottom and carry over the '1' to the next column along.
4) Add up the next column, including anything carried over: 3 + 4 + 0 + 1 = 8.
5) The last column just has a 2, so write this in.

So 3.74 + 24.2 + 0.6 = 28.54

...and Subtracting Decimals

E.g. Bob has £8, but spends 26p on bubble-gum. How much is left?

1) At first, this question doesn't look like it has any decimals in it. But we need both numbers in pounds — so it becomes £8.00 – £0.26.
2) Set it out as usual, making sure you LINE UP THE DECIMAL POINTS and put one in for the answer.
3) Look at each column from right to left, taking away the bottom number from the top.
4) Borrow 10 from the next column along if you need to, as before:

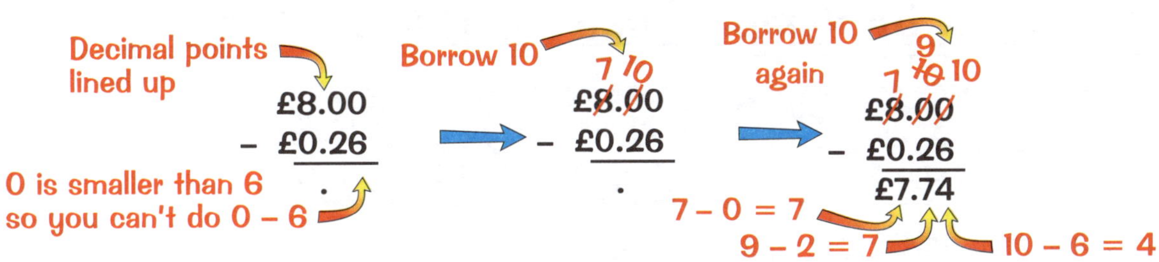

So £8.00 – £0.26 = £7.74.

Don't get short-changed — learn how to count your money...

In real life, you'll come across decimals most when dealing with money. Have a go at this question without using your calculator:

1) I want to buy a packet of sweets for 54p and a magazine for £2.30.
   a) How much will I have to pay in total? b) How much change will I have from a £5 note?

Multiplying by 10, 100, etc

You really should know the stuff on this page because:
a) it's really useful, and b) they're likely to test you on it in the exam.

1) To Multiply Any Number by 10

Move the Decimal Point ONE place RIGHT and fill any gaps with ZEROS.

EXAMPLES:

2 3.6 × 10
= 2 3 6

3 4 5 × 10
= 3 4 5 0

The gap's been filled with a zero.

2) To Multiply Any Number by 100

Move the Decimal Point TWO places RIGHT and fill any gaps with ZEROS.

EXAMPLES:

3 4 × 100
= 3 4 0 0

Gaps filled with zeros.

2.5 4 3 × 100
= 2 5 4 . 3

3) To Multiply by 1000 or 10 000

Move the Decimal Point so many places RIGHT and fill any gaps with ZEROS.

EXAMPLES:

3 4 1 × 1000
= 3 4 1 0 0 0

Gaps filled with zeros.

2.3 5 4 2 × 10 000
= 2 3 5 4 2

You always move the DECIMAL POINT this much:
1 place for 10, 2 places for 100,
3 places for 1000, 4 places for 10 000 etc.

4) To Multiply by Numbers like 20, 300, 8000, etc.

MULTIPLY by 2 or 3 or 8 etc. FIRST, then move the Decimal Point so many places RIGHT.

EXAMPLE: Find 234 × 2000.

1) First multiply by 2: 234 × 2 = 468
2) Then move the DP 3 places right: 468 × 1000 = 4 6 8 0 0 0

The gaps have been filled with zeros.

Go forth and multiply...

Four important methods to learn here. For a bit of a workout, try these without a calculator:

1) Work out a) 345 × 10 b) 12.3 × 100 c) 9.65 × 1000 d) 60 × 3000

Dividing by 10, 100, etc

This is useful stuff too. So make sure you know it — that's all.

1) To Divide Any Number by 10

Move the Decimal Point ONE place LEFT ( ) and if it's needed, REMOVE ZEROS after the decimal point.

EXAMPLES:

2 3.6 ÷ 10
= 2.3 6

3 4 0 ÷ 10
= 3 4.0
= 3 4

The zero after the decimal point has been removed.

2) To Divide Any Number by 100

Move the Decimal Point TWO places LEFT ( ) and REMOVE ZEROS after the decimal point.

EXAMPLES:

2 9 6.5 ÷ 100
= 2.9 6 5

3 4 0 ÷ 100
= 3.4 0
= 3.4

Zero removed.

3) To Divide by 1000 or 10 000

Move the Decimal Point so many places LEFT ( ) and REMOVE ZEROS after the decimal point.

You always move the DECIMAL POINT this much:
1 place for 10, 2 places for 100,
3 places for 1000, 4 places for 10 000 etc.

EXAMPLES:

2 3 5 0 0 ÷ 10 000
= 2.3 5 0 0
= 2.3 5 ← Zeros removed.

3 4 1 ÷ 1000
= 0.3 4 1

Fill in any gaps with zeros if you need to.

4) To Divide by Numbers like 40, 300, 7000, etc.

DIVIDE by 4 or 3 or 7 etc. FIRST, then move the Decimal Point so many places LEFT ( ).

EXAMPLE: Find 960 ÷ 300.

1) First divide by 3: 960 ÷ 3 = 320
2) Then move the DP 2 places left: 320 ÷ 100 = 3.20
3) You don't need the last zero after the decimal point, so the answer is 3.2.

Give this page your undivided attention...

Knowing how to divide by 10, 100, 1000, etc. will be very handy, so make sure you learn this page.

1) Work out (no calculators): a) 2.45 ÷ 10 b) 654.2 ÷ 100 c) 3.08 ÷ 1000 d) 32 ÷ 20

Multiplying Without a Calculator

You need to be able to multiply numbers together without a calculator — you'll have to do it in your Unit 2 exam. There are loads of ways to do it, but these two are pretty good.

E.g. Work out 46 × 27

The Grid Method

1) Split up each number into its units and tens (and hundreds and thousands if it has them). Look back at page 32 for how to do this.

46 = 40 + 6
27 = 20 + 7

2) Draw a grid, and split it up into how many 'bits' you've got. There are 4 bits here (40, 6, 20 and 7).

3) Write the 'bits' on the outside of the grid, like this:

	40	6
20		
7		

4) Multiply together the 'bits' on the edge of each square (the stuff on page 36 will help). Write each answer in the middle of each square.

	40	6
20	40 × 20 = 800	6 × 20 = 120
7	40 × 7 = 280	6 × 7 = 42

5) Add up all the numbers inside the squares (see page 34).

6) The total is your final answer.

```
  800
  120
  280
+  42
-----
 1242
  1
```

So: 46 × 27 = 1242

It helps if you know your times tables.

The 'Old' Way

— how old people would have learnt it at school.

I won't go into detail with this — the grid method's a lot easier to learn. But if you know how to do it this way then feel free to use it.

As you can see, the answer is the same either way.

```
    46
 ×  27
------
   3 2₄2   — This is 7 × 46
   9₁2 0   — This is 20 × 46
------
 1 2 4 2   — This is 322 + 920
```

46 × 27 = 1242

Dividing Without a Calculator

OK, time for dividing now. Don't worry — here's a tried-and-tested method you can learn...

The 'Short Division' Method

EXAMPLE: "What is 714 ÷ 21?"

1) Set out the division as shown, with the first number inside the box, and the second number on the outside.

```
21 | 7 1 4
```
This is where the answer will go.

2) The first number in the box is 7, so we say: "How many times will 21 go into 7?" The answer is 0 (because 21 is bigger than 7). So write a 0 over the 7 above the box.

```
     0
21 | 7 1 4
```
21 into 7 doesn't go.

3) 21 didn't go into 7, so we try the first two numbers together — 71. Count how many lots of 21 will fit into 71 (keep adding lots of 21 until you get there).

$21 + 21 = 42$
$42 + 21 = 63$
$63 + 21 = 84$ — too big
So $21 + 21 + 21 = 21 \times 3 = 63$

4) 21 will go into 71 3 times ($21 \times 3 = 63$) with 8 left over ($71 - 63 = 8$). So write the 3 above the box and carry the 8 (called a remainder) over to the next number as shown.

```
     0 3
21 | 7 1 ⁸4
```
Carry the 8.

21 into 71 goes 3 times, remainder 8.

5) Look at the last number, including the 8 carried over — this gives 84. Count how many lots of 21 will fit into 84. You should find that it fits exactly 4 times with no remainder, so write the 4 above the box as shown.

```
     0 3 4
21 | 7 1 ⁸4
```
21 into 84 goes 4 times exactly.

6) The number on top of the box is your final answer. (You can ignore the zero at the start.)

So 714 ÷ 21 = 34.

Sums without calculators — less painful than standing on a plug barefoot...

Lots to take in there — it's really important that you learn the methods on these two pages though. Unless you know a different way that always works — in which case it's fine to use that. Read the last two pages again if you're still a bit unsure. Then try all of these without a calculator:

1) 28×12 2) 56×11 3) 104×8 4) 321×56
5) $242 \div 2$ 6) $84 \div 7$ 7) $96 \div 8$ 8) $275 \div 11$

Multiples, Factors and Primes

Hmm, the words above look important. Panic not — help is on its way...

Multiples

The MULTIPLES of a number are just its TIMES TABLE.

E.g: The multiples of 4 are: 4 8 12 16 20 24 28 32 36 ...
The multiples of 9 are: 9 18 27 36 45 54 63 72 ...

Factors

The FACTORS of a number are all the numbers that DIVIDE INTO IT.

E.g. 8 goes exactly into 32, so we say that 8 is a factor of 32.

You might be asked to find ALL the factors of a number — here's how to do it:

EXAMPLE: Find ALL the factors of 24.

1) Start off with 1 × the number itself: 1 × 24 = 24.
2) Then try 2 × something to make 24.
   2 × 12 = 24, so this is the next row.
3) Now try 3 × something, and so on, listing the pairs in rows.
4) Try each one in turn and put a dash if it doesn't divide exactly.
5) Eventually, when you get a number repeated, you stop.

Increasing by 1 each time

1 × 24
2 × 12
3 × 8
4 × 6
~~5 × –~~
6 × 4

So the FACTORS OF 24 are 1, 2, 3, 4, 6, 8, 12, 24

PRIME Numbers Don't Divide by Anything

1) Prime Numbers are all the numbers that DON'T come up in Times Tables (other than their own):

2 3 5 7 11 13 17 19 23 29 31 37 ...

2) The only way to get ANY PRIME NUMBER is: 1 × ITSELF

E.g: The only numbers that multiply to give 7 are: 1 × 7
The only numbers that multiply to give 31 are: 1 × 31

Two is the oddest prime of all — it's the only one that's even...

Learn all three sections on this page, then cover the stuff above and have a go at these:

1) List the first 10 multiples of 6, and the first 10 multiples of 7.
2) List all the factors of 36.
3) Write down the first 10 prime numbers (without looking).

Special Number Sequences

You need to know all the number sequences on the next two pages.
They're all special in their own way. Bless. Here we go with the first few...

EVEN Numbers all Divide by 2

2 4 6 8 10 12 14 16 18 20...

1) All EVEN numbers END in 0, 2, 4, 6 or 8, e.g. 200, 342, 576, 94.

2) So any number that ends in one of these is EVEN, and can be DIVIDED BY 2.

ODD Numbers Don't Divide by 2

1 3 5 7 9 11 13 15 17 19 21 ...

Everyone thought 3 was a little odd.

1) All ODD numbers END in 1, 3, 5, 7 or 9, e.g. 301, 95, 807, 43.

2) So any number that ends in one of these is ODD, and CAN'T be divided by 2.

SQUARE Numbers:

1) They're called SQUARE NUMBERS because they're like the areas of this pattern of squares:

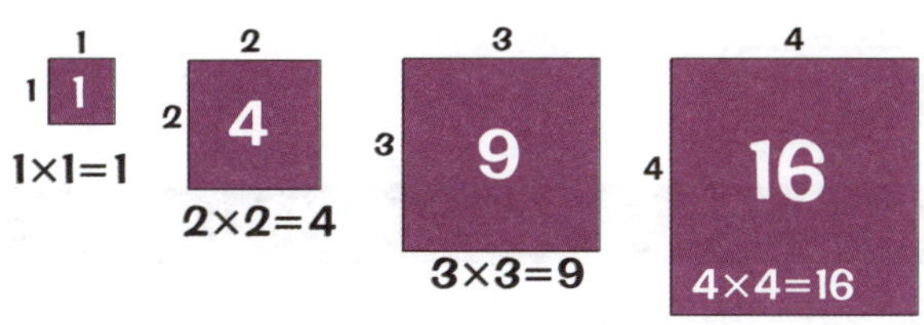

Areas are covered in Unit 3 (page 73).

(1×1)	(2×2)	(3×3)	(4×4)	(5×5)	(6×6)	(7×7)	(8×8)	(9×9)	(10×10)	(11×11)	(12×12)	(13×13)	(14×14)	(15×15)
1	4	9	16	25	36	49	64	81	100	121	144	169	196	225...

Differences: 3, 5, 7, 9, 11, 13, 15, 17, 19, 21, 23, 25, 27, 29

2) Note that the DIFFERENCES between the square numbers are all the ODD numbers.

Special Number Sequences

And now for the rest. Remember, these sequences are just as special.

CUBE Numbers:

They're called CUBE NUMBERS because they're like the volumes of this pattern of cubes:

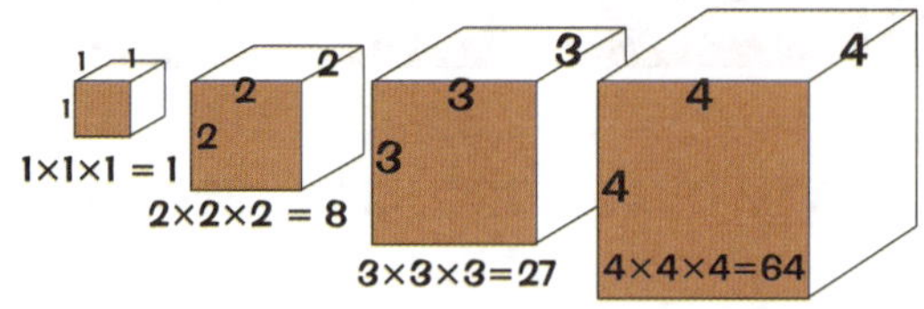

Volume is covered in Unit 3 (page 75).

(1×1×1)	(2×2×2)	(3×3×3)	(4×4×4)	(5×5×5)	(6×6×6)	(7×7×7)	(8×8×8)	(9×9×9)	(10×10×10)...
1	8	27	64	125	216	343	512	729	1000...

POWERS:

1) Powers are 'numbers multiplied by themselves so many times'.
2) For example: 'Two to the power three' = $2^3 = 2 \times 2 \times 2 - 8$

The First Few POWERS OF 2:

2	4	8	16	32...
$2^1=2$	$2^2=4$	$2^3=8$	$2^4=16$	etc...

To get the next number in the sequence, just times the last one by 2.

The First Few POWERS OF 10:

10	100	1000	10 000	100 000...
$10^1=10$	$10^2=100$	$10^3=1000$	etc...	

To get the next number in the sequence, just add an extra zero to the end of the last one.

What do you do if your cube numbers are sad? Tell them they're special...

1) Cover up the last 2 pages and then write down the first 10 numbers in all six sequences.
2) From this list of numbers: 23, 45, 56, 81, 25, 97, 134, 156, 125, 36, 64
write down: a) all the even numbers b) all the odd numbers c) all the square numbers
d) all the cube numbers e) all the powers of 2

Square Roots

Take a deep breath, and get ready for this page. Good luck with it, I'll be rootin' for ya...

Square Roots

1) 'Squared' means 'times by itself' : $P^2 = P \times P$.
2) SQUARE ROOT is the reverse of this:

'Square Root' means
'What Number Times by Itself gives...'

EXAMPLE 1: Find the square root of 49 (written as 'find $\sqrt{49}$')
To do this you should say "what number times by itself gives 49?".
$7 \times 7 = 49$, so $\sqrt{49} = 7$.

EXAMPLE 2: Find $\sqrt{100}$
Say "what number times by itself gives 100?".
$10 \times 10 = 100$, so $\sqrt{100} = 10$.

It will help a lot if you know the square numbers off by heart — see page 41.

Square Roots can be Positive or Negative

1) When you take the square root of a number, the answer can actually be positive or negative.
2) You always have a positive and negative version of the same number.

E.g. The square roots of 4 are $+\sqrt{4}$ and $-\sqrt{4}$, which are equal to +2 and −2

3) To understand why, try squaring both +2 and −2:

$$2^2 = 2 \times 2 = 4 \quad \text{but also} \quad (-2)^2 = (-2) \times (-2) = 4$$

'−' × '−' always gives '+'. See page 49 for how to multiply negative numbers.

1) You're not allowed a calculator in Unit 2, but for other units you can find square roots on your calculator using the SQUARE ROOT BUTTON, [√].
E.g. press [√] [49] [=] 7

2) Your calculator will only give you the POSITIVE square root.
It's up to you to REMEMBER to give the negative one as well.

Have a look at page 4 if you're not sure what buttons do what on your calculator.

Cube Roots

Just like square rooting is the reverse of squaring, cube rooting is the reverse of... cubing.

Cube Roots

1) 'Cubed' means 'times by itself three times' : $T^3 = T \times T \times T$.

2) CUBE ROOT is the reverse of this:

Well, strictly there are only two × signs, but you know what I mean.

'Cube Root' means 'What Number Times by Itself THREE TIMES gives...'

3) Unlike square roots, there's only ever one answer for cube roots.

   Cube roots of positive numbers are always POSITIVE.

   Cube roots of negative numbers are always NEGATIVE.

Notice the little 3.

EXAMPLE: Find the cube root of 64 (written as 'find $\sqrt[3]{64}$')

You should say "What number times by itself three times gives 64?"
This is not always as obvious as for square roots, so take a few guesses:

Try $3^3 = 3 \times 3 \times 3 = 27$ (Too small...)

Try $5^3 = 5 \times 5 \times 5 = 125$ (Too big...)

Try $4^3 = 4 \times 4 \times 4 = 64$ (Just right!)

So if $4^3 = 64$, then the answer is $\sqrt[3]{64} = 4$.

The number is positive, so the cube root is positive too.

For Units 1 and 3, you can use the cube root button on your calculator (if it has one):

Press [∛] [64] [=] 4

"Cue brute" — that's what they call me when I play snooker...

LEARN the methods for finding square roots and cube roots on the last 2 pages.
Then give these questions a go:

1) If $g^2 = 36$, write down both answers for g (i.e. find $+\sqrt{36}$ and $-\sqrt{36}$).

2) If $b^3 = 27$, find b (i.e. find $\sqrt[3]{27}$).

Fractions, Decimals and Percentages

Fractions, decimals and percentages are three different ways of showing a proportion (or part) of something. Read on to learn how to switch between them.

You met fractions and percentages in Unit 1 (p.7-10).

Fractions You Should Know

This table shows the proportions you should know straight off, without having to work them out:

Fraction	Decimal	Percentage
$\frac{1}{2}$	0.5	50%
$\frac{1}{4}$	0.25	25%
$\frac{3}{4}$	0.75	75%
$\frac{1}{3}$	0.33333... or $0.\dot{3}$	$33\frac{1}{3}\%$
$\frac{1}{10}$	0.1	10%
$\frac{2}{10}$	0.2	20%
$\frac{1}{5}$	0.2	20%

This is called a recurring decimal — the 3 keeps repeating itself forever.

How to Switch Between Them

For proportions not in the table above, use these flowcharts to help switch between the three types:

Fraction —(Divide top by bottom)→ Decimal —(× by 100)→ Percentage

Fraction ←(Use the columns (see example 2 below))— Decimal ←(÷ by 100)— Percentage

EXAMPLE 1: $\frac{2}{5}$ is: $2 \div 5 = 0.4$ as a decimal, and $0.4 \times 100 = 40\%$ as a percentage.

See p.36 for doing this without a calculator.

See p.37 for doing this without a calculator.

EXAMPLE 2: 30% is: $30 \div 100 = 0.3$ as a decimal.

The 3 is in the tenths column, so it's 'three tenths' or $\frac{3}{10}$ as a fraction.

If the fraction's not in its simplest form you need to cancel down — see page 7.

Oh, what's recurrin'?...

Knowing all of the top table and the flowchart will help you loads in the exam.

1) Turn the following decimals into fractions and percentages: a) 0.7 b) 0.01 c) 0.6

Fractions

You'll need to do calculations with fractions without your calculator. Here's how...

Multiplying

1) Multiply the top numbers to make the new top number (numerator)...
2) ...and multiply the bottom numbers to make the new bottom number (denominator).

E.g. $\frac{3}{5} \times \frac{4}{7} = \frac{3 \times 4}{5 \times 7} = \frac{12}{35}$

Dividing

1) Turn the 2nd fraction UPSIDE DOWN...
2) ...and then multiply, as shown above.

E.g. $\frac{3}{4} \div \frac{1}{3} = \frac{3}{4} \times \frac{3}{1} = \frac{3 \times 3}{4 \times 1} = \frac{9}{4}$

2nd fraction is now upside down.

Adding and Subtracting

1) If the bottom numbers are the same, add or subtract TOP NUMBERS ONLY, leaving the bottom number as it is.

E.g. adding: $\frac{2}{6} + \frac{1}{6} = \frac{2+1}{6} = \frac{3}{6}$ and subtracting: $\frac{5}{7} - \frac{3}{7} = \frac{5-3}{7} = \frac{2}{7}$

2) If the bottom numbers are different, you have to make them the same using equivalent fractions (see page 7).

E.g. to do $\frac{1}{2} + \frac{1}{4}$, turn the $\frac{1}{2}$ into $\frac{2}{4}$ and then add as usual: $\frac{2}{4} + \frac{1}{4} = \frac{2+1}{4} = \frac{3}{4}$

Ordering Fractions — Put Them Over the Same Number

E.g. Which is bigger, $\frac{2}{3}$ or $\frac{3}{4}$?

$\frac{2}{3} = \frac{8}{12}$ (×4 top and bottom) $\qquad \frac{3}{4} = \frac{9}{12}$ (×3 top and bottom)

1) Look at the bottom numbers ('denominators') of the fractions: 3 and 4.
2) Think of a number they will both go into — try 12.
3) Change each fraction (make equivalent fractions) so the bottom number is 12.
4) Now check which is biggest by looking at their top numbers ('numerators').
5) 9 is bigger than 8, so $\frac{3}{4}$ is bigger than $\frac{2}{3}$.

'The Denominator' — maths robot from the future...

Now you've learnt these useful tips, it's time to have a go at these below — without a calculator.

1) a) $\frac{3}{4} \times \frac{5}{6}$ b) $\frac{4}{5} \div \frac{7}{8}$ c) $\frac{3}{8} + \frac{1}{8}$ d) $\frac{4}{5} - \frac{2}{5}$ e) $\frac{3}{10} + \frac{2}{5}$

2) Which is bigger, $\frac{3}{5}$ or $\frac{2}{3}$?

Ratios

You met ratios in Unit 1 (see p.11-12), so this GOLDEN RULE might seem familiar...

DIVIDE FOR ONE, THEN TIMES FOR ALL

Example:

"The milkman delivers skimmed and full fat milk in the ratio 5:2.
If there are 6 bottles of full fat, how many bottles of skimmed are there?"

1) The GOLDEN RULE says: **DIVIDE FOR ONE, THEN TIMES FOR ALL**

2) In the ratio, there are 5 parts skimmed to 2 parts full fat.
So the 6 bottles of full fat must be worth 2 parts.

3) To find how many bottles is ONE PART, DIVIDE the number of bottles of full fat by 2.

   6 bottles ÷ 2 parts = 3 bottles (for one part)

4) Then MULTIPLY by 5 to find how many bottles of skimmed there are.

   3 bottles × 5 parts = 15 bottles of skimmed (for 5 parts).

Splitting Into Ratios

Sometimes you need to SPLIT AN AMOUNT into a certain RATIO.

EXAMPLE: "£5000 is to be divided in the ratio 1:4. Find the two amounts."

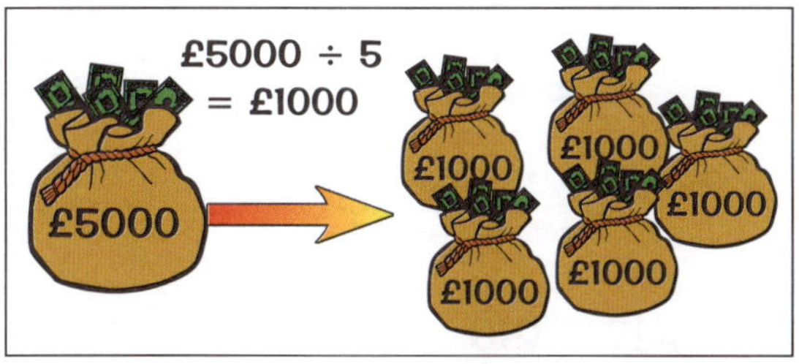

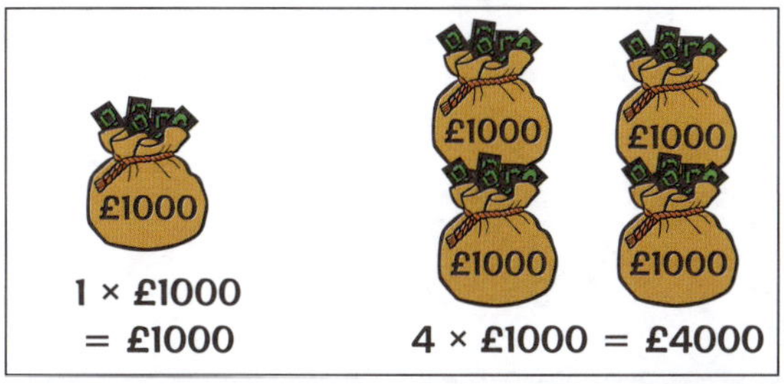

1) £5000 is split into 5 equal parts (because 1 + 4 = 5).

   £5000 ÷ 5 parts = £1000 per part

2) The first person in the ratio 1:4 gets 1 part...

   1 × £1000 = £1000

3) ...and the second person gets 4 parts.

   4 × £1000 = £4000

4) So the two amounts are £1000 and £4000.

One rule to... er... rule them all...

Learn the examples above and put your skills to the test with these questions.

1) Chris and Steve have ages in the ratio 3:4. If Chris is 18, how old is Steve?
2) Divide £2400 in the ratio 5:7.

Revision Test for Unit 2 — 1

DON'T use your calculator for these questions.

1) Write this number out in words: 1 306 515

2) Put these numbers in order of size, smallest to biggest:
   a) 23 6534 123 2200 2 132 789 45
   b) 0.01 0.12 0.003 0.05 0.6 0.0021

3) Work out: a) 756 + 328 + 61 b) 456 – 291 c) 8.63 + 2.1 + 0.4

4) Alvin wants to buy a pet fish (costing £6.45) and some fish food (costing £1.34).
   a) How much will this cost in total?
   b) How much change will he have from £10.00?

5) Jan needs to buy 100 large envelopes at £1.20 each. How much money does she need?

   Hint: 1.20 × 100.

6) Chris bought 100 chocolate bars for £32 to sell in the school tuck shop. How much should he sell each chocolate bar for to make his money back?

   Hint: 32 ÷ 100.

7) Work out: a) 69×11 b) $145 \div 5$

8) Find the first six multiples of 10.

9) Find all the factors of 30.

10) What are square numbers? Write down the first five of them.

11) Find all possible answers of: a) The square root of 225 b) $\sqrt[3]{216}$.

12) What is 40% as: a) a decimal? b) a fraction?

13) Work out: a) $\frac{2}{3} \times \frac{2}{5}$ b) $\frac{5}{6} \div \frac{8}{3}$ c) $\frac{5}{8} + \frac{2}{8}$ d) $\frac{5}{9} - \frac{3}{9}$

14) Which is bigger, $\frac{7}{8}$ or $\frac{3}{4}$?

15) Grandma Wolfe has £800 to split between her two grandchildren in the ratio 1:3. How much does each child get?

Negative Numbers

Negative numbers are just numbers less than zero. You might come across them on a freezing day, when the temperature drops. Or possibly on your bank statement if you've spent too much...

Rules For Multiplying and Dividing

1) When doing calculations you have to watch out for the signs of the numbers: positive (+) or negative (–).
2) The signs in the question can affect the sign of the answer, like so:

> Positive numbers are numbers more than zero. We don't usually bother putting the positive sign (+) before them, so if a number hasn't got a sign, it must be positive.

+	+	makes	+
+	–	makes	–
–	+	makes	–
–	–	makes	+

3) BUT this ONLY works in the following TWO CASES:

1) MULTIPLYING or DIVIDING

E.g:
$-2 \times 3 = -6$
(– and + makes answer –)

E.g:
$-8 \div -2 = +4\ (= 4)$
(– and – makes answer +)

2) When two signs appear NEXT TO each other

E.g:
$5 - -4 = 5 + 4 = 9$

Two – signs together can be changed to one + sign.

E.g:
$4 + -6 - -7 = 4 - 6 + 7 = 5$

– and – together changed to one +.

+ and – together changed to one –.

These aren't next to each other so don't combine them.

Use a Number Line To Add Or Subtract

For calculations involving ADDITION AND SUBTRACTION, use a NUMBER LINE:

E.g. "Work out 4 – 8 – 3 + 6"

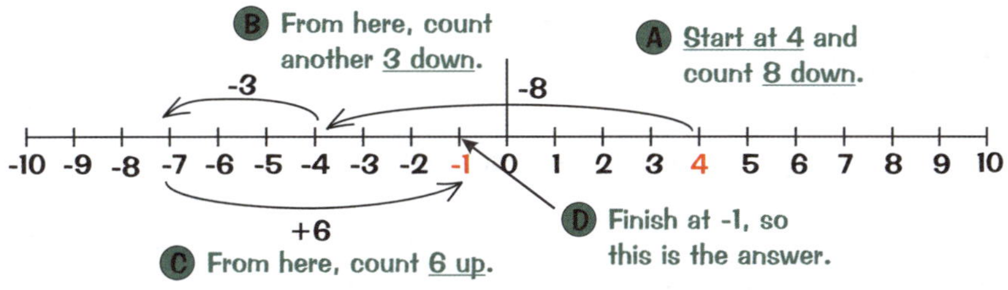

So 4 – 8 – 3 + 6 = -1

Now stop being so negative — this stuff's not so bad...

Most of the time you follow the rules without thinking — because we usually work with positive numbers where the signs never change. Learn everything on the page, then try these without a calculator:

1) Work out a) -4×-3 b) $-4 + -5 + 3$ c) $12 \div -4$ d) $(3 + -2 - 4) \div (2 + -5)$

Powers and Letters

Right. LEARN THIS PAGE, then PEEL ME SOME GRAPES and IRON MY SHIRTS.
Sorry, I think the power's gone to my head...

Powers Make Things Look Tidier

1) As you saw on page 42, a power tells you how many times a number is multiplied by itself.
2) Powers are written like this:

2^7 means 'two to the power 7' = 2×2×2×2×2×2×2

6^5 means 'six to the power 5' = 6×6×6×6×6

7^2 means 'seven to the power 2' or '7 squared' = 7×7

4^3 means 'four to the power 3' or '4 cubed' = 4×4×4

There are 7 lots of 2 multiplied together.

See pages 41-42 for more on square and cube numbers.

Letters Can Be Multiplied Together

1) ALGEBRA is using letters to stand for numbers.
2) Sometimes we use a letter because we don't know the number.
3) Sometimes we use a letter to stand for any number.
4) Either way, you can usually treat the letters as if they were numbers.
5) With algebra, there are a few rules which tell you how to make things look a bit simpler:

LEAVE OUT '×' SIGNS BETWEEN LETTERS:

- 'abc' means 'a×b×c'.
- Write '2 × n' as just '2n'.
- Write numbers before letters, so 'g × 4' is '4g' NOT 'g4'.

LETTERS CAN HAVE POWERS TOO:

- 'a^4' means 'a × a × a × a'
- 'gn^2' means 'g×n×n'. (Note that only the n is squared, not the g as well).

BRACKETS CAN HELP LUMP BITS TOGETHER:

- '$(gn)^2$' means 'g×g×n×n'. The ^{2} is outside the brackets so BOTH letters are squared.
- '$(q - r)^2$' means '(q − r) × (q − r)'.
- '-3^2' means $-(3 \times 3) = -9$, BUT $(-3)^2$ means $-3 \times -3 = 9$.

When we tidy things up like this it's called simplifying.

"I've got the power! oh, oh, oh, oh..." Oh no, I'm feeling kinda 90s...

I hope all that algebra stuff hasn't put you off. It makes life simpler for maths teachers, but it can seem pretty scary for the rest of us. Learn this page, then try simplifying these using the rules:

1) a) 3 × 3 × 3 × 3 b) 4 × 4 × 4 c) a × a × a × a × a d) 3 × a × b × b e) b × b × 7

Algebra — Simplifying

Algebra really scares so many people. But honestly, it's not that bad. You've just got to make sure you understand and learn these basic rules for dealing with algebra. After that, all it needs is practice, practice, practice... and a little love.

Terms

You need to understand what a TERM is:

1) **A TERM IS A GROUP OF NUMBERS, LETTERS AND BRACKETS, ALL MULTIPLIED OR DIVIDED TOGETHER.**

2) Terms are SEPARATED BY + AND – SIGNS e.g. $4x^2 - 3py - 5 + 3p$

   Four different terms.

3) Terms always have a + or – ATTACHED TO THE FRONT OF THEM.

4) e.g. (4xy) (+ $5x^2$) (– 2y) (+ $6y^2$) (+ 4)

   Invisible + sign — 'xy' term, 'x^2' term, 'y' term, 'y^2' term, 'number' term

5) When terms are grouped together like this, it's called an EXPRESSION.

Simplify Expressions By Collecting Like Terms

1) To simplify an expression, collect together all the terms that have the same letter or group of letters in them — called 'LIKE TERMS'.

2) Numbers on their own are 'like terms' because they all have 'no letters' in.

EXAMPLE: Simplify the expression: $2x - 4 + 5x + 6$

(2x) (–4) (+5x) (+ 6) = (+2x) (+5x) (–4) (+6)

Invisible + sign; x-terms; number terms

= 7x +2 = 7x + 2

1) Put bubbles round each term — including the +/– sign IN FRONT of each.

2) Move the bubbles so that LIKE TERMS are together.

3) Combine LIKE TERMS by adding or subtracting.

   So $2x + 5x = x + x + x + x + x + x + x = 7x$. AND $-4 + 6 = +2$.

   (2 lots of x, 5 lots of x, 7 lots of x)

   (Use a number line to help — p.49)

4) So $2x - 4 + 5x + 6$ simplifies to: $7x + 2$.

Algebra — Brackets

Multiplying Out Brackets

We use brackets with numbers to say which part of a calculation should be done first (see p.3).

It's a bit different with algebra — you're often asked to 'MULTIPLY OUT' or 'EXPAND' an expression with a bracket in. Here's how:

To EXPAND a bracket, multiply the bit on the outside with everything on the inside.

EXAMPLE 1: Expand $3(2x + 5)$

This means $3 \times (2x + 5)$, so multiply the '2x' by 3, and the '+5' by 3 too:

$$3(2x + 5) = 6x + 15$$

$3 \times 2x$ 3×5

LEARN THESE TWO RULES:

1) When letters are multiplied together, they are written next to each other (in alphabetical order), or as powers. E.g. $p(q + p) = p \times q + p \times p = pq + p^2$.
2) A minus outside the bracket REVERSES ALL THE SIGNS when you multiply.

EXAMPLE 2: $4p(3r - 2t) = 12pr - 8pt$

$4p \times 3r$ $4p \times -2t$

EXAMPLE 3: $-4(3p - 7q) = -12p + 28q$

$-4 \times 3p$ $-4 \times -7q$

Note both signs have been reversed — Rule 2. The $+3p$ became $-12p$, and the $-7q$ became $+28q$.

1) You can also be asked to FACTORISE an expression — this means putting brackets back in.
2) To factorise, look at what will go into both terms and put this outside a bracket.

E.g. factorise the expression $5a + 10$:
5 will go into both terms so put 5(   ).
Then find something to go inside the bracket that will make $5a + 10$ when you multiply it out:
$5(a + 2)$ multiplies out to give $5a + 10$, so $5a + 10 = 5(a + 2)$.

Go forth and multiply out brackets...

Learn all the key facts on the last 2 pages, then have a go at these questions to see if you've got it.

1) Simplify: a) $5x + 3y - 4 - 2y - x$ b) $3x + 2 + 5xy + 6x - 7$

2) Expand: a) $2(x - 2)$ b) $x(5 + x)$ c) $y(y + x)$ d) $3y(2x - 6)$

Formulas

A formula is a way of giving instructions without using loads of words.
So instead of saying "Square a number, times it by 7 and take away 11", say $N = 7x^2 - 11$. Nice.

Substitution — Putting Numbers In

Algebra uses letters in place of numbers.
Sometimes you're asked to put the numbers BACK IN — this is called SUBSTITUTION.

EXAMPLE: Substitute $x = 10$ into the expression $3x + 2$.

METHOD:

1) Think about what the expression is telling you to do to 'x' and write it out in full.
   Here we have to times 'x' by 3 and add 2: $3 \times x + 2$.

2) Put the number in place of the letter.
   Here, $x = 10$, so: $3 \times 10 + 2$.

3) Finally, work out the value: $3 \times 10 + 2 = 30 + 2 = 32$.

Use BODMAS (p.3) to work things out in the right order.

When Using Formulas, Do One Bit at a Time...

Substituting numbers into formulas is just the same.
They might look tricky, but take it step by step.

Example: Temperature can be measured in degrees Celsius (°C) or degrees Fahrenheit (°F).

We can use the formula: $F = \frac{9}{5}C + 32$ to swap between the two.

If the temperature is 15 °C ($C = 15$), find the temperature in degrees Fahrenheit (°F).

Method:

1) Write out the formula in full $\qquad F = \frac{9}{5} \times C + 32$

2) Write it again, but put numbers in place of any letters you know.
   Here you're told that $C = 15$. $\qquad F = \frac{9}{5} \times 15 + 32$

   See p.7

3) Work it out IN STAGES.
   WRITE DOWN values for each bit as you go along.

$F = 27 + 32$

$F = 59$

So 15 °C = 59 °F

There's no substitute for a bit of hard work I'm afraid...

There's no getting out of it, you'll have to learn everything on this page. Then have a crack at these:

1) Substitute $x = 2$ into these expressions: a) $5x + 15$ b) $10x - 7$ c) $\frac{1}{2}x + 4$
2) Use the formula $A = 2C - 6$ to find A when $C = 9$.

Making Formulas from Words

You need to know the "tricks of the trade" for making formulas from words.
There are two main types:

Type 1:

Where you have instructions about what to do with a number and you have to write it as a formula.
The instructions can be any one of these (where 'x' stands for a number):

1) Multiply x 2) Divide x 3) Square or square root x (x^2 or $\sqrt{x}$)
4) Cube x (x^3) 5) Add or subtract a number

Example 1: "To find y, subtract four from x"

Answer: Start with x $\rightarrow$ $x - 4$ (Subtract 4) so $y = x - 4$

Example 2: "To find y, divide x by three and then subtract seven. Write a formula for y."

Answer: Start with x $\rightarrow$ $\frac{x}{3}$ (Divide it by 3) $\rightarrow$ $\frac{x}{3} - 7$ (Subtract 7) So $y = \frac{x}{3} - 7$

Type 2:

Where you have to make up a formula by putting in letters
like 'C' for 'cost' or 'n' for 'number of something-or-others'.

Example: 'CHOCCO-BURGERS' cost 58 pence each. Write a formula for the total cost, T, of buying n 'CHOCCO-BURGERS' at 58p each.

Answer: T stands for the total cost
n stands for the number of 'CHOCCO-BURGERS'

In WORDS the formula is: Total Cost = Number of 'CHOCCO-BURGERS' × 58p
Putting the LETTERS in: $T = n \times 58$ or to write it better: $T = 58n$

I love this page SO MUCH that words fail me...

Nope. I got nothin'. Best just do these questions:

1) y is found by multiplying x by five and then subtracting three.
Write down a formula for y in terms of x.
2) Reindeer kebabs cost 95p each.
Write a formula for the total cost, C pence, of buying n kebabs.

Solving Equations

The 'proper' way to solve equations is shown on the next page.
The 'proper' way can sometimes be hard though — so there are some easier methods shown below.
The problem with these is that you can't always use them on very tricky equations.
In most exam questions though, they do just fine.

1) The 'Common Sense' Way

1) The unknown 'x' is just a number.
2) The 'equation' is just a clue to help you find out what the number is.

Example: "Solve this equation: $3x + 4 = 46$"
(i.e. find what number x is)

Answer: This is what you should say to yourself:

"Something + 4 = 46" hmm, so that 'something' must be 42. ← Because 42 + 4 = 46.

So that means $3x = 42$, which means '3 times something = 42'.

So it must be $42 \div 3$ which is 14 so $x = 14$.

And doing a final check gives $3 \times 14 + 4 = 46$, so it must be right.

2) The Trial and Error Way

1) This works best if the answer is a whole number.
2) In the trial and error method, you find a number that's too big, and a number that's too small, and then try values in between them.

Example: "Solve for x: $3x + 5 = 11$"
(i.e. find out what number x is)

Answer:

Try $x = 1$: $(3 \times 1) + 5 = 3 + 5 = 8$ — no good, it's too small (we want 11)

Try $x = 3$: $(3 \times 3) + 5 = 9 + 5 = 14$ — no good, it's too big

SO TRY IN BETWEEN: $x = 2$: $(3 \times 2) + 5 = 6 + 5 = 11$, YES, so $x = 2$.

But I'm innocent your honour — this trial is an error...

~~Loan those two methods~~. No. ~~Learn these to meatheads~~. No. Learn these two methods. Splendid.
Now use either one of them to answer these:

1) Solve: $4x + 12 = 20$ 2) Solve: $5x - 9 = 6$

Solving Equations

The 'proper' way of solving equations isn't too difficult, it just needs lots of practice.

3) The 'Proper' Way

GOLDEN RULES FOR SOLVING EQUATIONS

1) Always do the SAME THING to both sides of the equation.
2) To get rid of something, do the opposite.
   The opposite of + is − and the opposite of − is +.
   The opposite of × is ÷ and the opposite of ÷ is ×.
3) Keep going until you have a letter on its own.

Example 1: Solve $5x = 15$

$5x = 15$
$x = 15 \div 5$
$\underline{x = 3}$

5x means 5 × x, so do the opposite — divide both sides by 5.

Example 2: Solve $\frac{p}{3} = 2$

$\frac{p}{3} = 2$
$p = 2 \times 3$
$\underline{p = 6}$

$\frac{p}{3}$ means p ÷ 3, so do the opposite — multiply both sides by 3.

Example 3: Solve $4y - 3 = 17$

For equations like this you'll need to do it in two steps.

$4y - 3 = 17$
$4y = 20$
$\underline{y = 5}$

1) The opposite of −3 is +3 — so add 3 to both sides.
2) The opposite of ×4 is ÷4 — so divide both sides by 4.

Example 4: Solve $2(x + 3) = 11$

For questions with brackets you might have to use three steps.

$2(x + 3) = 11$
$2x + 6 = 11$
$2x = 5$
$\underline{x = 2.5}$

1) Multiply out the brackets (p.52). Now you can solve it like Example 3.
2) The opposite of +6 is −6 — so subtract 6 from both sides.
3) The opposite of ×2 is ÷2 — so divide both sides by 2.

This page could solve all your algebra problems...

If you can solve equations the 'proper' way then you might as well get good at it.
This way you'll be able to solve any equation on the exam, instead of just hoping you get an easy one...

1) Solve these equations: a) $3x = 18$ b) $\frac{q}{4} = 8$ c) $3x + 1 = 13$ d) $5(y + 2) = 20$

Number Patterns and Sequences

With number patterns, you need to be able to work out the rule for getting the next number in the sequence. There are five different types that you need to be able to find the rule for.

FINDING THE RULE FOR EXTENDING THE PATTERN MEANS...

WORK OUT WHAT YOU DO TO THE PREVIOUS TERM TO GET TO THE NEXT TERM

1) 'Add or Subtract the Same Number'

The SECRET is to WRITE THE DIFFERENCES IN THE GAPS between each pair of numbers:

E.g. 2 5 8 11 14 ... (gaps: +3 +3 +3 +3 +3)   30 24 18 12 ... (gaps: -6 -6 -6 -6)

The RULE: 'Add 3 to the previous term'   'Subtract 6 from the previous term'

2) 'Add or Subtract a Changing Number'

Again, WRITE THE CHANGE IN THE GAPS, as shown here:

E.g. 8 11 15 20 26 ... (gaps: +3 +4 +5 +6 +7)   or   53 43 34 26 19 ... (gaps: -10 -9 -8 -7 -6)

The RULE: 'Add 1 extra each time to the previous term'   'Subtract 1 less from the previous term'

3) Multiply by the Same Number each Time

This type has the same number MULTIPLYING the previous number in the pattern each time:

E.g. 5 10 20 40 ... (gaps: ×2 ×2 ×2 ×2)   2 6 18 54 ... (gaps: ×3 ×3 ×3 ×3)

The RULE: 'Multiply the previous term by 2'   'Multiply the previous term by 3'

Number Patterns and Sequences

Just two more patterns to go...

4) Divide by the Same Number each Time

This type have the same number DIVIDING the previous number each time:

E.g. 400 200 100 50 ... (÷2 ÷2 ÷2 ÷2)   40 000 4000 400 40 ... (÷10 ÷10 ÷10 ÷10)

The RULE: 'Divide the previous term by 2'   'Divide the previous term by 10'

5) Add the Previous Two Terms

This type of sequence works by ADDING THE LAST TWO NUMBERS to get the next one.

E.g. 1 1 2 3 5 8 13 ... (1+1 1+2 2+3 3+5 5+8 8+13)   2 4 6 10 16 ... (2+4 4+6 6+10 10+16)

This sequence is a pretty special one known as the FIBONACCI SEQUENCE. You don't need to know that for your exam, but if you're ever on a game show and it's the £1 000 000 question, be sure to look me up and thank me.

The RULE: 'Add the previous two terms'

"LEARN THIS PAGE, LEARN THIS PAGE..." — I can see a pattern here...

The first thing to do when faced with a sequence is to work out the differences between the numbers. If that doesn't help, check if they're being multiplied or divided by a number instead. If that still fails, try adding together two numbers next to each other and see if you come out with the next one in the sequence. You might also be asked to carry on the sequence using the rule.

Learn the last 2 pages, then write down the rules and find the next number in the pattern for these:

1) a) 21 19 17 15 13 11 ...   b) 1 2 4 7 11 16 ...   c) 2 20 200 2000 20 000 ...

2) a) 64 32 16 8 4 2 ...   b) 9 10 19 29 48 77 ...

X and Y Coordinates

Graph questions can be fun. OK, maybe not fun, but better than being out in a hail storm in just your pants. First, you need to know the basics...

Plot Coordinates On a Grid

1) You draw graphs on a grid, a bit like this one.
2) It's made by two lines crossing — called the axes.
3) The y-axis goes from bottom to top, and the x-axis goes from left to right.
4) They meet at the point with coordinates (0, 0) — this is called the origin.
5) Coordinates are a pair of numbers that tell us where a point is on the grid.
6) The x-coordinate tells us how far along, and the y-coordinate tells us how far up to draw a point.
7) To plot (draw) a graph, plot coordinates first then join them up.

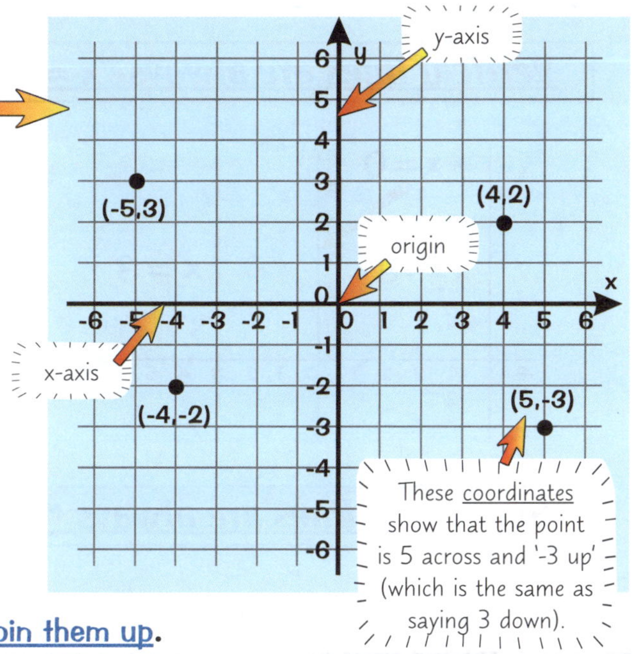

X, Y Coordinates — Getting them in the Right Order

1) You must always give coordinates in brackets like this: (x, y)
2) And you always have to be really careful to get them the right way round, x first, then y.
3) Here are three ways you could remember:

(x , y)

1) The two coordinates are always in ALPHABETICAL ORDER, x then y.
2) x is always the flat axis going ACROSS the page. In other words 'x is a...cross' Get it — x is a '×'. (Hilarious isn't it.)
3) Remember it's always IN THE HOUSE (→) and then UP THE STAIRS (↑) so it's ALONG first and then UP, i.e. x-coordinate first, and then y-coordinate.

But what if you live in a bungalow?...

In that case, you just have to imagine where the stairs would be. So, make sure you learn one of the 3 Rules for getting x and y the right way round. Then turn over and see what you can remember.

1) Write down the coordinates of the letters A to H on this graph:

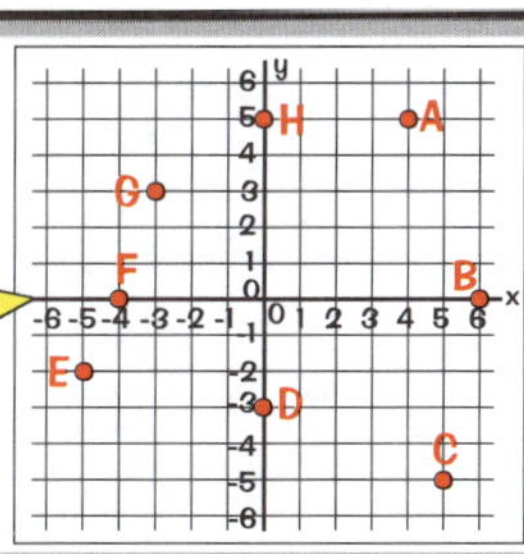

Straight-Line Graphs

If you thought I-spy was fun, wait until you play 'spot the graph from its equation'.

Horizontal and Vertical Lines: E.g. x = 3 and y = –2

Vertical lines are always "x = a number"

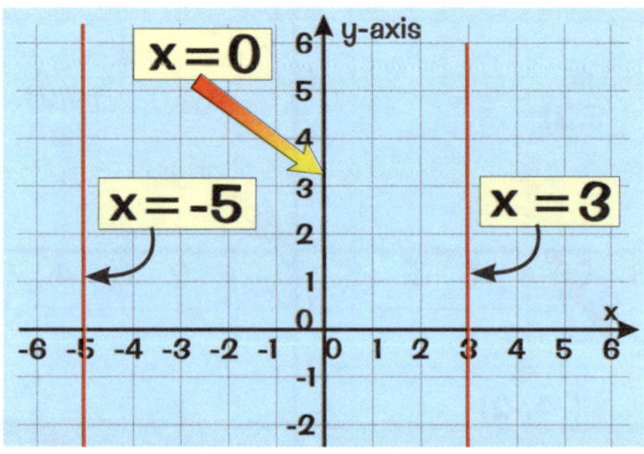

1) E.g. $x = -5$ is a vertical line through '-5' on the x-axis.
2) The y-axis is also the line $x=0$.

Horizontal lines are always "y = a number"

1) E.g. $y = 3$ is a horizontal line through '3' on the y-axis.
2) The x-axis is also the line $y=0$.

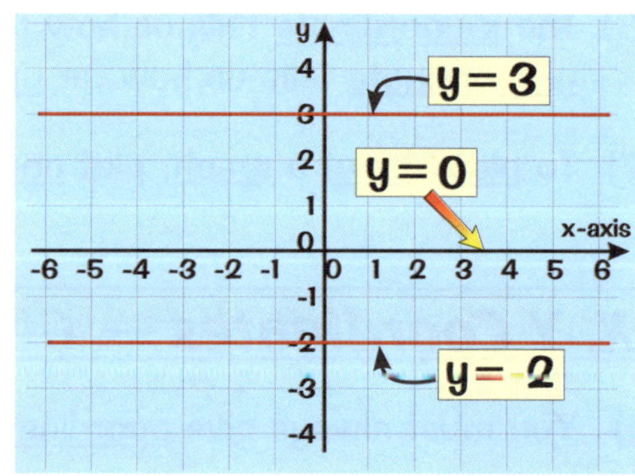

The Main Diagonals: "y = x" and "y = –x"

Both these lines go through the origin (0, 0).

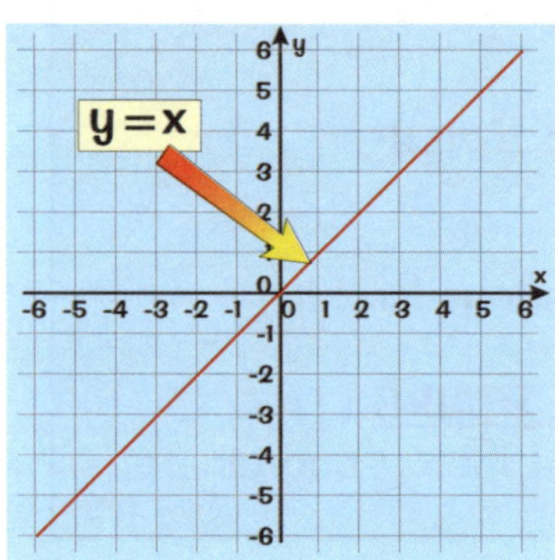

'$y = x$' is the main diagonal that goes UPHILL from left to right.

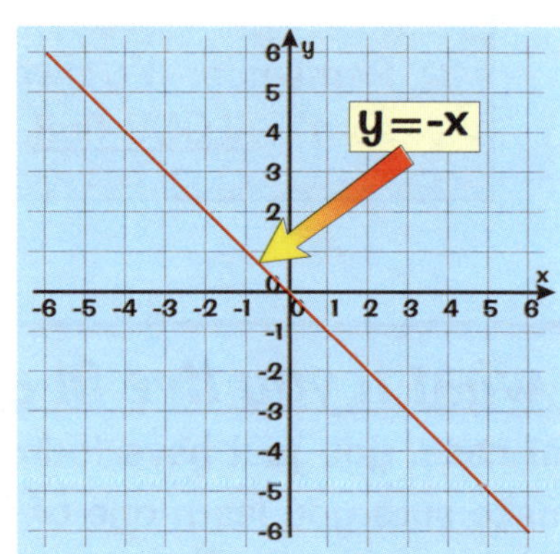

'$y = -x$' is the main diagonal that goes DOWNHILL from left to right.

There are more sloping lines on the next page...

Straight-Line Graphs

Joy of joys, here are more graphs to learn...

Other Sloping Lines Through the Origin: "y = ax" and "y = –ax"

$y = ax$ and $y = -ax$ are equations for **SLOPING LINES THROUGH THE ORIGIN** (where 'a' is just a number).

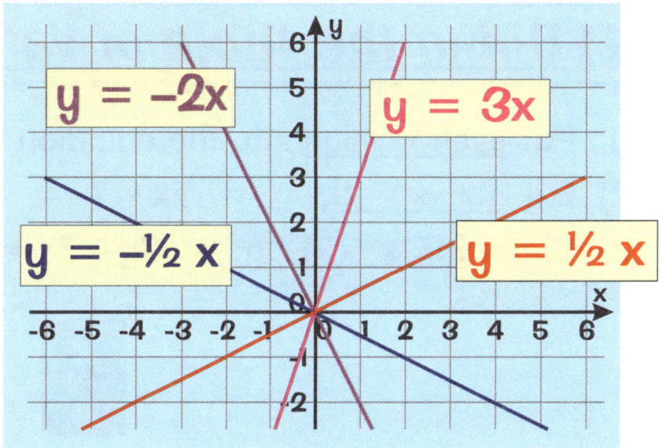

1) The value of 'a' (known as the gradient) tells you the steepness of the line.
2) The bigger 'a' is, the steeper the slope. E.g. the line $y = 3x$ on the right is steeper than $y = \frac{1}{2}x$, because 3 is bigger than ½.
3) A MINUS SIGN tells you it slopes DOWNHILL. E.g. $y = -2x$ and $y = -\frac{1}{2}x$ both slope downhill.

All Other Straight Lines

1) Other straight-line equations are a little more tricky.
2) The next page shows you how to draw them, but the first step is spotting them in the first place.
3) STRAIGHT-LINE EQUATIONS just have 'SOMETHING X, SOMETHING Y, AND A NUMBER'.
4) If an equation has things like x^2 (or other powers), xy or $\frac{1}{x}$, then it's NOT A STRAIGHT LINE.

It doesn't have to have all of these bits (e.g. $x = 2$ is still a straight line) but straight lines won't have anything other than these bits.

EXAMPLES:

Straight lines:

$x - y = 0$	$y = 2 + 3x$
$2y - 4x = 7$	$4x - 3 = 5y$
$3y + 3x = 12$	$6y - x - 7 = 0$

NOT straight lines:

$y = x^3 + 3$	$2y - \frac{1}{x} = 7$
$\frac{1}{y} + \frac{1}{x} = 2$	$x(3 - 2y) = 3$
$x^2 = 4 - y$	$xy + 3 = 0$

My favourite line's y = 3x, it gets the chicks every time...

OK, maybe not every time, but it's still worth learning all this stuff.
When you think you know it, turn over the page and see what you can remember.

Straight-Line Graphs

Strap on a beret, grab a pencil and let's get arty (well, graphy at least) — it's graph drawing time. In the exam, you'll probably get a table to fill in, and be asked to plot a graph from an equation.

EXAMPLE: Complete this table of values, using the equation $y = 2x - 7$, and use it to plot a graph of $y = 2x - 7$.

x	-2	0	2	4	6
y	-11		-3		

1) Doing the Table of Values

1) Put each x-value into the equation and work out the matching y-values.
2) E.g. for $x = 0$, $y = 2x - 7 = (2 \times 0) - 7 = 0 - 7 = -7$ ...
3) ...and for $x = 4$, $y = 2x - 7 = (2 \times 4) - 7 = 8 - 7 = 1$ etc. until you get:

x	-2	0	2	4	6
y	-11	-7	-3	1	5

2) Plotting The Points and Drawing The Graph

1) PLOT EACH PAIR of x- and y-values CAREFULLY from the table as a point on the graph.
2) The points will form A DEAD STRAIGHT LINE.
3) Draw a line through them with a RULER.

x	-2	0	2	4	6
y	-11	-7	-3	1	5
(x,y)	(-2,-11)	(0,-7)	(2,-3)	(4,1)	(6,5)

These are the coordinates you need to plot.
Look back at page 59 if you need to.

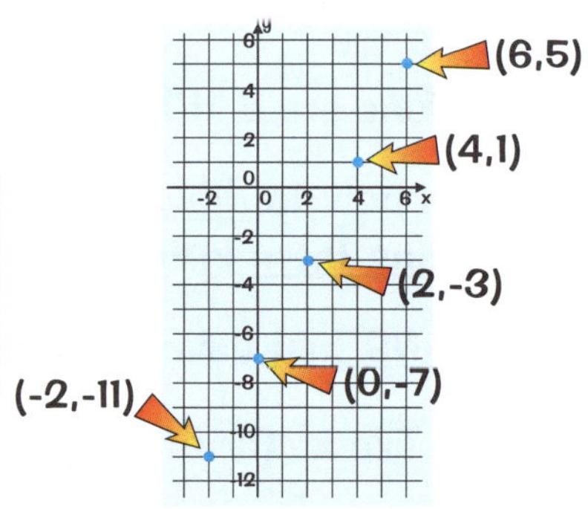

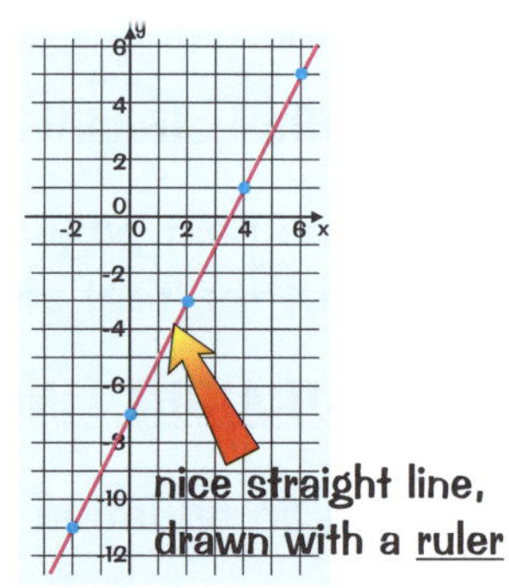

4) NEVER let one point stick out from the rest. You should never get SPIKES on a straight-line graph.

5) If one point does look a bit odd, check 2 things:
   a) the y-value you worked out in the table
   b) that you've plotted it properly.

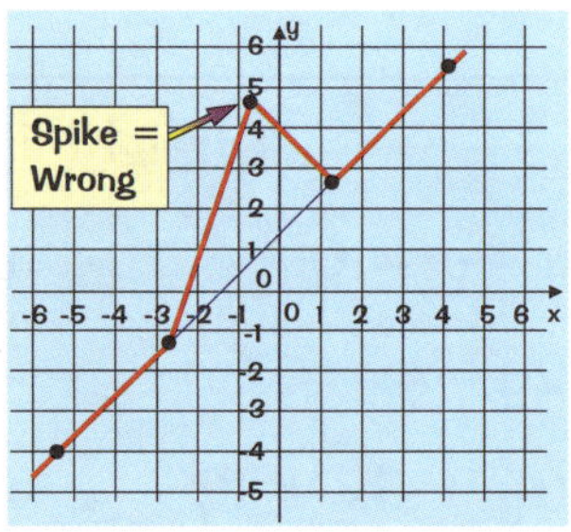

Careful plotting — the key to perfect graphs and being an evil genius...

... mwah ha ha ha. Learn this page, then have a go at the questions below.

1) Complete this table of values for the equation: $y = x - 2$
2) Then plot the points on graph paper and draw the graph.

x	-4	-2	-1	0	1	2	4
y	-6			-2			

Travel Graphs

Yay, just what you wanted to see — some more graphs...

Know What Travel Graphs Show

1) A TRAVEL GRAPH shows DISTANCE (↑) against TIME (→) for a MOVING OBJECT (e.g. a car, person, goat...).
2) FLAT SECTIONS show where the object has STOPPED.
3) The STEEPER the graph the FASTER it's going.
4) The graph GOING UP means it's travelling AWAY.
5) The graph COMING DOWN means it's COMING BACK AGAIN.

Example: Travel Graph For A Cyclist...

EXAMPLE: The travel graph below shows the journey of Sarah, out on a bike ride. Explain what's happening at each stage of Sarah's journey.

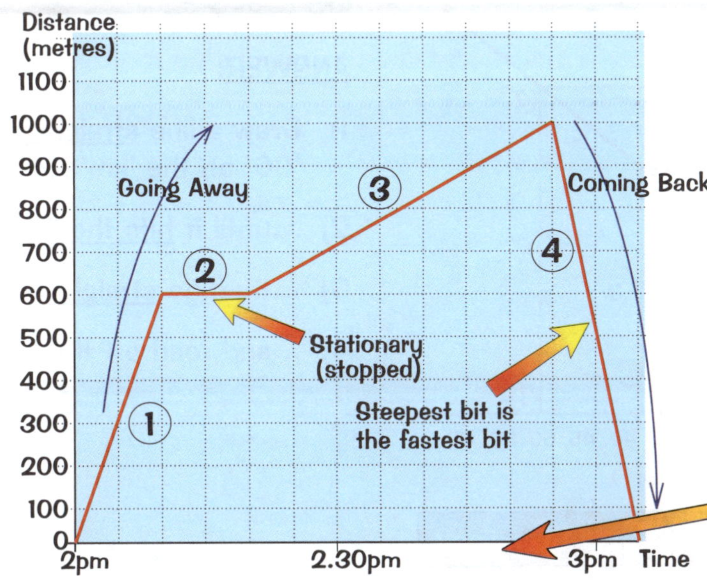

There are 12 squares between 2pm and 3pm — so each square must be 60 ÷ 12 = 5 mins.

1) Sarah rides 600 m away from her house at a steady speed for 10 mins.
2) She stops for a 10 minute rest (flat means 'stopped')
3) She carries on for 35 mins, doing another 400 m — she's now 1000 m from her house. She's going slower on this bit — you can tell because the graph isn't as steep.
4) In this last bit, Sarah rides the full 1000 m back to her house in one go, in 10 mins. She's going fastest on this bit — you can tell because the graph is steepest here.

Learning maths is just like riding a bike...

...except without the grazed knees when you fall off. The trick is — once you've learnt it, you'll find it a lot easier to remember how to do it again, in the exam say. So start pedalling and learn this page...

Conversion Graphs

In the exam you might get a question with a conversion graph which helps you switch between different units — for things like money (£ → Dollars) or speed (mph → km/h) etc.

Know How to Read Off Conversion Graphs

1) Draw a line from the VALUE YOU KNOW on one axis.
2) Keep going until you hit the LINE.
3) Then CHANGE DIRECTION and go straight to the other axis.
4) READ OFF THE NEW VALUE from the axis. That's the answer.

Example: Conversion Graph For Distances

This graph converts between miles and kilometres:

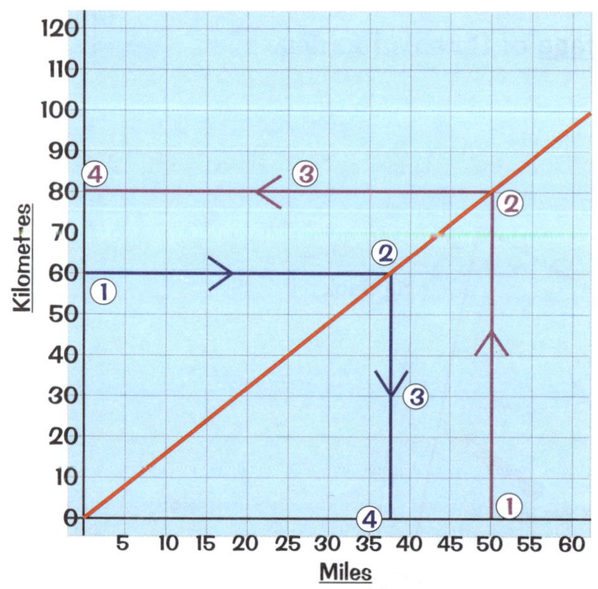

EXAMPLE 1: How many miles is 60 km?

ANSWER:

1) Draw a line straight across from '60' on the 'km' axis...
2) ...until it hits the line...
3) ...then go straight down to the 'miles' axis...
4) ...and read off the answer: 37.5 miles

EXAMPLE 2: How many km is 50 miles?

ANSWER:

1) Draw a line straight up from '50' on the 'miles' axis...
2) ...until it hits the line...
3) ...then go straight across to the 'km' axis...
4) ...and read off the answer: 80 km

Convert this page into exam marks...

You might hear about "ready reckoner" graphs — these are just conversion graphs that make it easy to do calculations, so treat them just the same. You'll need to learn this page first though.

Reading off Graphs

It doesn't matter what type of graph you get — distance and time, chickens and aliens — to read values from a graph you just need to follow the same method every time.

Getting Answers From Your Graph

FOR A SINGLE CURVE OR LINE, you ALWAYS get the answer by:

1) drawing a straight line to the graph from one axis,
2) and then down or across to the other axis.

Example:

The graph shows the height of a ball as it is thrown through the air.
Use the graph to find the approximate times when the ball was 1 m above the ground.

Approximate just means you don't have to be exact, just give roughly the right answer.

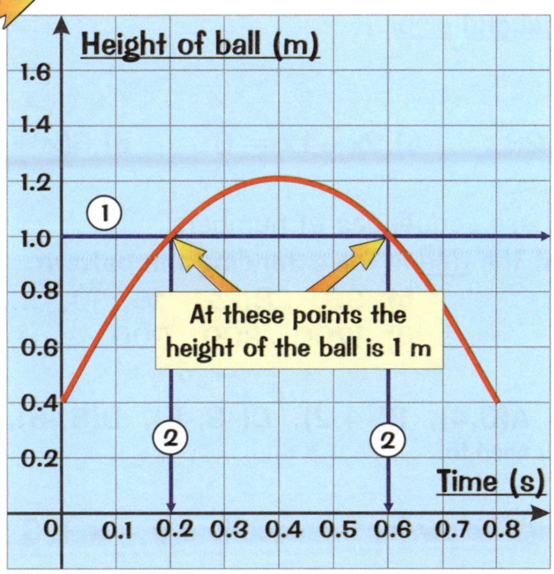

METHOD:

1) Draw a straight line across the graph at 1.0 on the vertical ↑ axis ('height of ball') — this is where the height of the ball is 1 m.

2) This line crosses the graph twice.
Draw straight lines down to the horizontal → axis ('time') at these points and read off the values:

Time = 0.2 s and 0.6 s.

ANSWER: So the ball was 1 m above the ground at 0.2 s and 0.6 s.

Right graph — we're not leaving here 'til I get some answers...

Learn the rules for getting answers from your graph. Then turn over... you know what to do by now...

Revision Test for Unit 2 — 2

1) Work out: a) -3×-2 b) -4×8 c) $12 \div -4$ d) $-20 \div -4$

2) Simplify: a) $4 \times n \times n \times n$ b) $a \times a \times 2$

3) Simplify the expression: $3x + 4y + 2x - y$

Don't forget to look for any invisible + signs.

4) Expand these expressions: a) $4(3g + 5h - 1)$ b) $x(x - 6)$

5) Ellen's thermometer only measures in Celsius (°C) but her dad can only understand temperatures in Fahrenheit (°F). She knows that to get a temperature in °F you need to 'times the temperature in °C by $\frac{9}{5}$ and then add 32'.

a) Write out a formula for changing °C into °F.
b) Use your formula to find the temperature in Fahrenheit when it is 30 °C.

Use the letter C for the temperature in °C and F for the temperature in °F.

6) Find x if $x^2 = 81$. (Use trial and error.)

7) Solve these equations:
a) $x + 3 = 7$ b) $4x = 28$ c) $2x - 12 = 6$ d) $5(x + 5) = 10$

8) Find the next two terms in these sequences of numbers.
For each sequence, say what the rule is for extending the pattern.
a) 3, 7, 11, 15, ..., ... b) 36, 28, 21, 15, 10, ..., ...
c) 3, 6, 12, 24, ... , ... d) 1200, 600, 300, ..., ...

9) Plot these points on a grid: A(0,4), B(-4,2), C(-3,-5), D(5,-6), E(5,0).
Copy the grid from page 59 if you need to.

10) a) Complete the table of values below for the equation: $y = x + 3$
b) Draw the graph.

x	-5	-3	-1	0	1	2	4	6
y	-2				4			

11) The travel graph on the right shows the journey of a goat walking along a road.
Describe what the goat is doing:
a) Between 4 pm and 6 pm.
b) Between 6 pm and 7 pm.
c) How far from home does the goat stray?

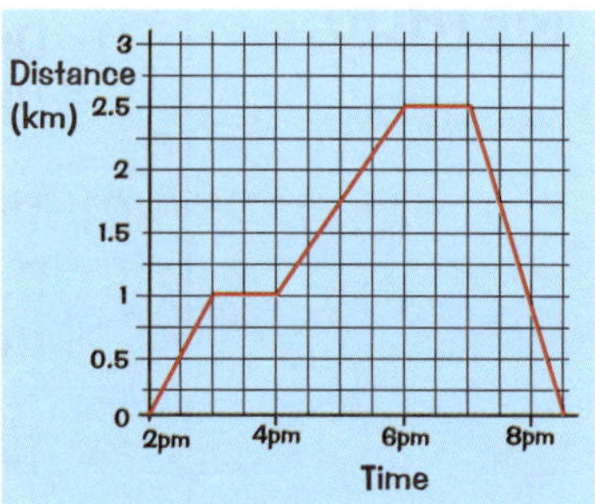

12) At the market, Farmer Miles can trade in his sheep for chickens.
This conversion graph helps him find what the animals are worth.
How many chickens can he get for 10 sheep?

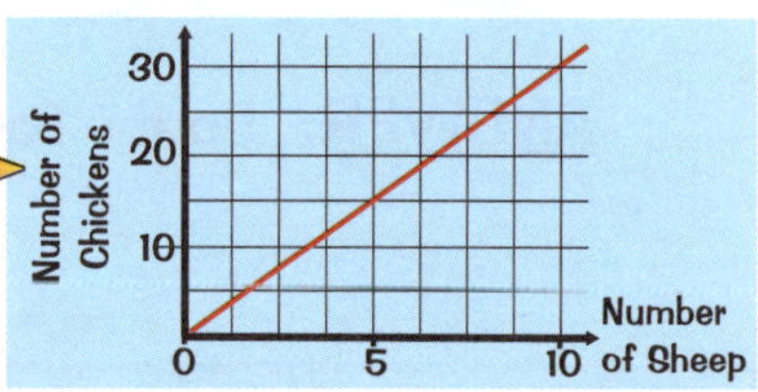

Symmetry

There are TWO types of symmetry, and guess what — you need to know about them both.

1) Line Symmetry is...

...where you draw a MIRROR LINE across a picture and both sides will fold exactly together.

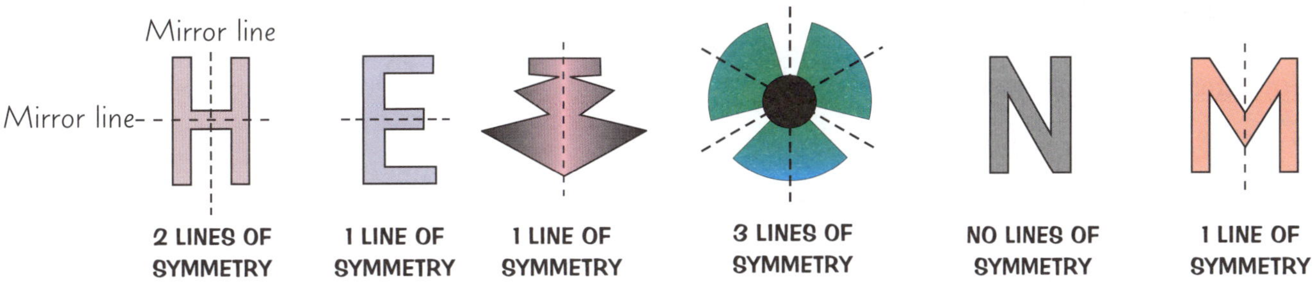

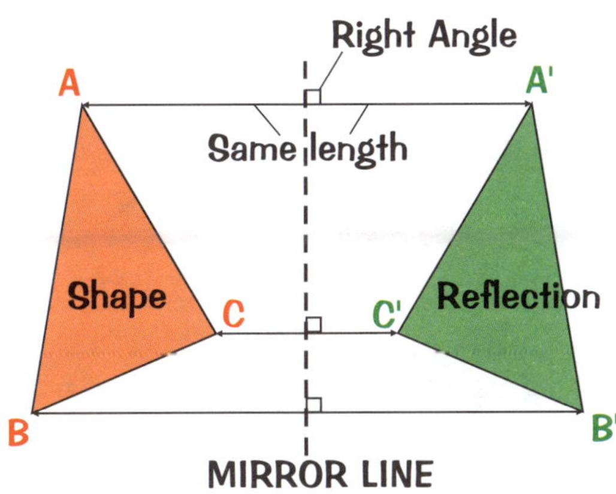

How to Draw a Reflection:

1) Label each corner of the shape (e.g. A, B, C...)
2) From point A, draw a line at right angles to the mirror line.
3) Carry on the line to the other side of the mirror line.
4) Mark a point at exactly the same distance away from the mirror line as A. Call this A'.
5) Repeat for all the other points.
6) Join up the points (A', B' and C') to make the reflection.

2) Rotational Symmetry is...

...where you turn (rotate) a shape around into different positions that all look exactly the same.

1) The 'order' means how many different positions look the same.
2) For 'order 1', only one position is the same. It has no rotational symmetry.

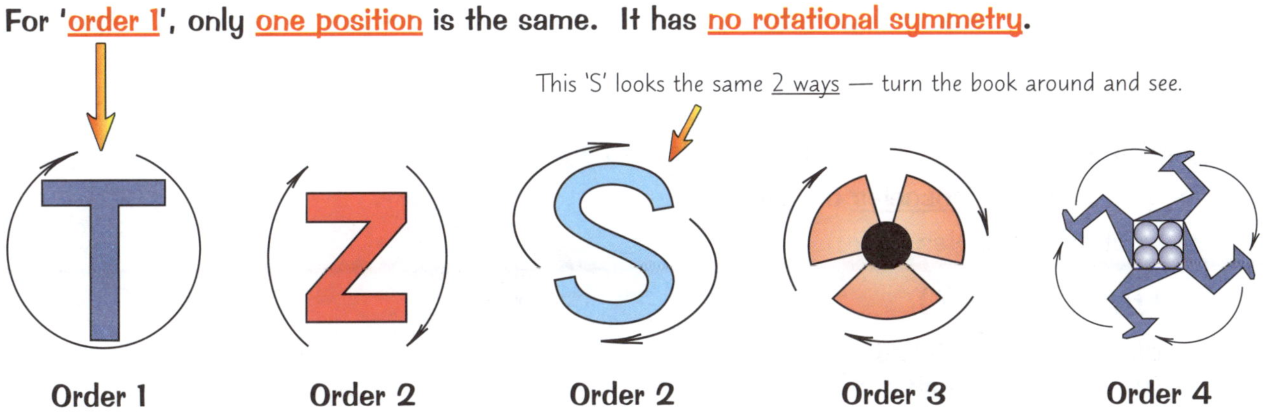

2D Shapes

2D shapes are flat shapes. There are loads of different types, and they're special in different ways (just like your mates). Make sure you know all the ones on the next two pages.

Three-sided Shapes — Triangles

1) Equilateral

Equilateral triangles have:

- All 3 sides the same length.
- All 3 angles the same — 60°.
- 3 lines of symmetry.
- Rotational symmetry order 3 (see p.67).

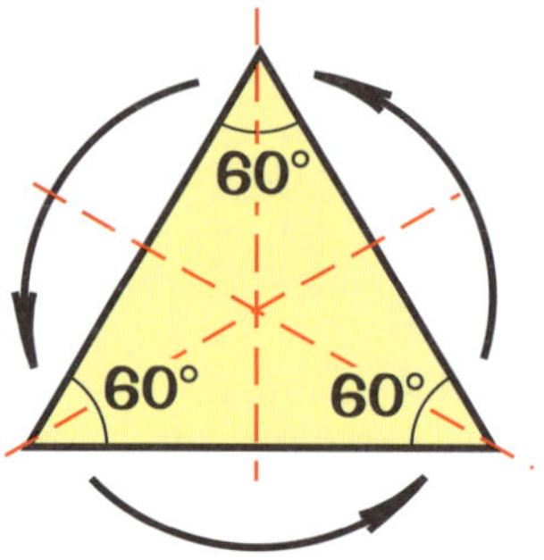

2) Isosceles

Isosceles triangles have:

- 2 sides the same length.
- 2 angles the same.
- 1 line of symmetry.
- No rotational symmetry (order 1).

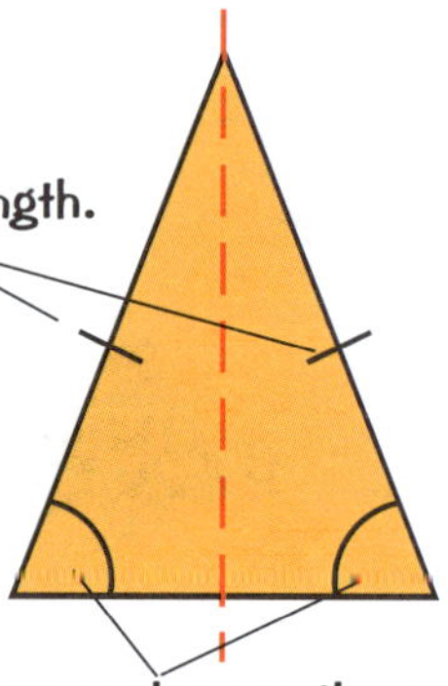

3) Scalene

Scalene triangles are just triangles that aren't special like the others.

- All three sides different lengths.
- All three angles different.
- No symmetry.

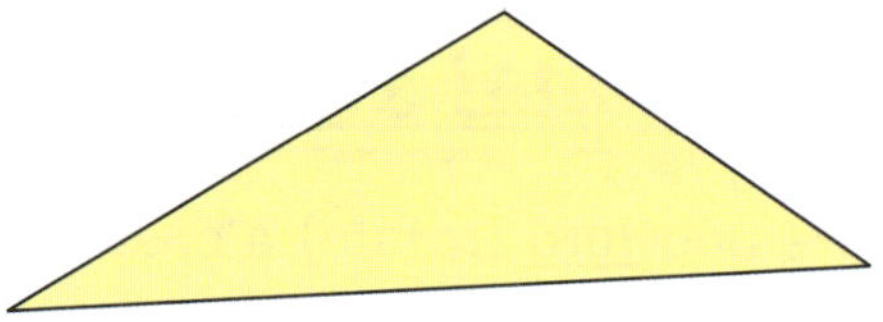

4) Right-Angled

1) Right-angled triangles have a right-angle (90°) somewhere.
2) They can also be isosceles or scalene.
3) Right-angled triangles have:
   - 1 right angle (90°).
   - No lines of symmetry (unless it's isosceles too).
   - No rotational symmetry (order 1).

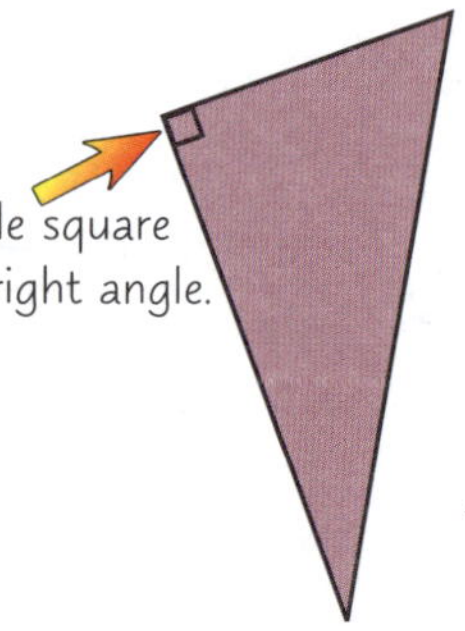

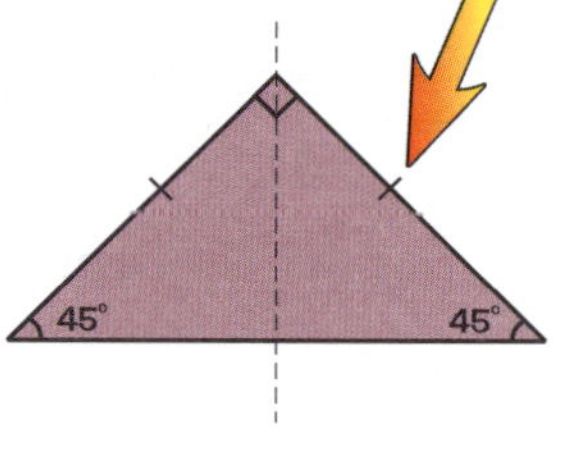

2D Shapes

Four-sided Shapes — Quadrilaterals

1) SQUARE

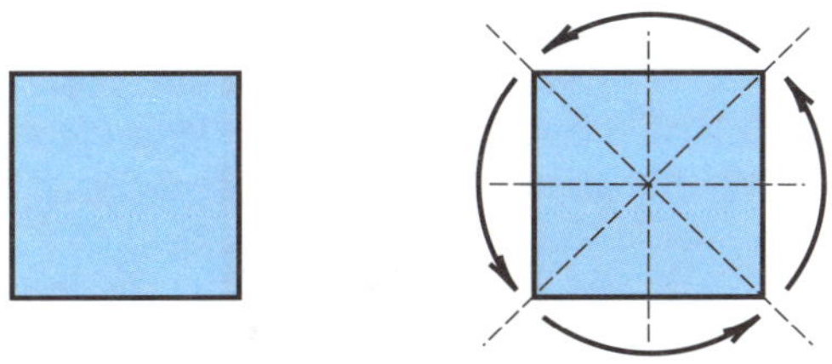

- All sides the same length.
- All angles the same (90°).
- 4 lines of symmetry.
- Rotational symmetry order 4.

2) RECTANGLE

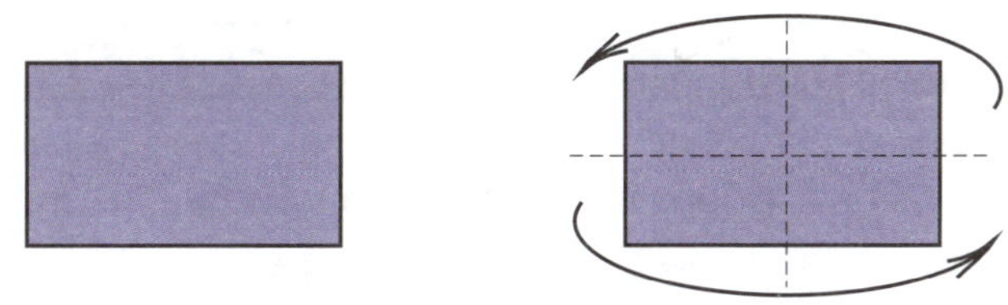

- 2 pairs of sides the same length.
- All angles the same (90°).
- 2 lines of symmetry.
- Rotational symmetry order 2.

3) RHOMBUS

(A square pushed over.)

These arrows mean parallel sides (see p.77).

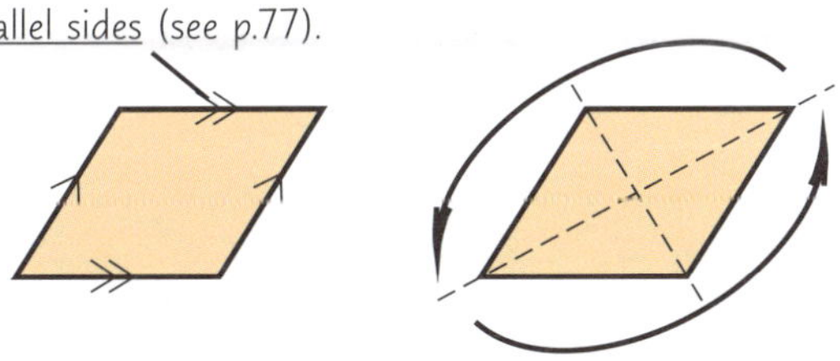

- All sides the same length.
- 2 pairs of parallel sides.
- 2 lines of symmetry.
- Rotational symmetry order 2.

4) PARALLELOGRAM

(A rectangle pushed over.)

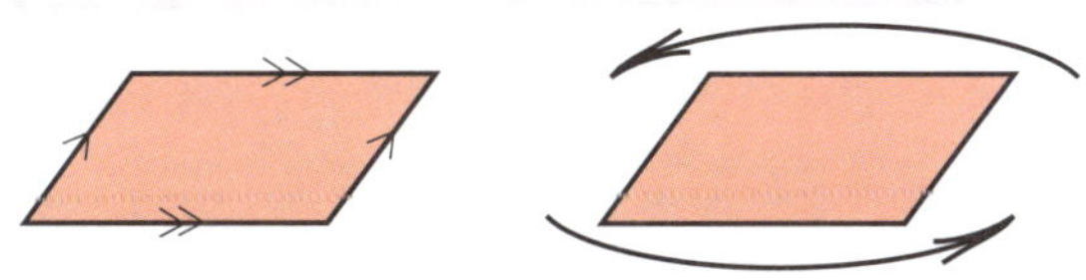

- 2 pairs of sides the same length.
- 2 pairs of parallel sides.
- NO lines of symmetry.
- Rotational symmetry order 2.

5) TRAPEZIUM

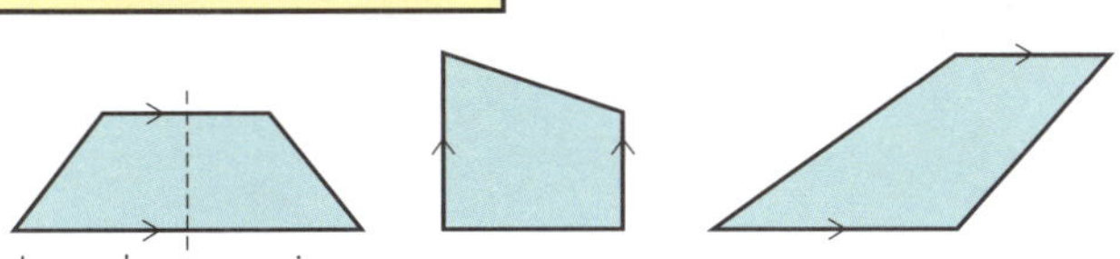

Isosceles trapezium

- One pair of parallel sides
- Only the isosceles trapezium has a line of symmetry.
- None have rotational symmetry.

6) KITE

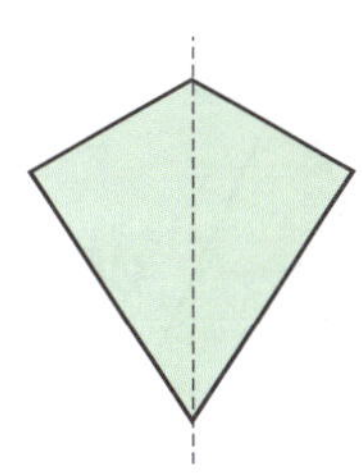

- 1 line of symmetry.
- No rotational symmetry.

Rhombus facts: 4 sides, 2 lines of symmetry, Gemini, peanut allergy...

Learn everything on these pages. Then turn over and say all the details that you can remember. Then try again. It's as simple as that. Then you can play with the kite. Indoors though — it's new.

3D Shapes

I was going to make some pop-out 3D shapes to put on this page, but I couldn't find the scissors and sticky tape. Sorry.

3D Shapes Are Solid Shapes

Some 3D Shapes Are Called Prisms:

1) A prism is a 3D shape which has the same sized shape running all the way through it.
2) E.g. if you slice up a cylinder (like slicing a cucumber) the end face of each slice will be the same — a circle.
3) We say that prisms have a 'constant area of cross-section'.

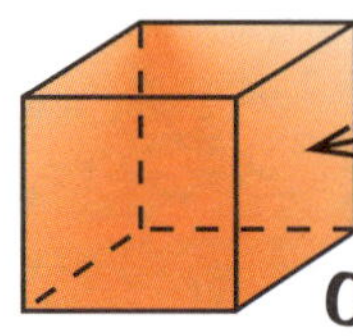

CUBE

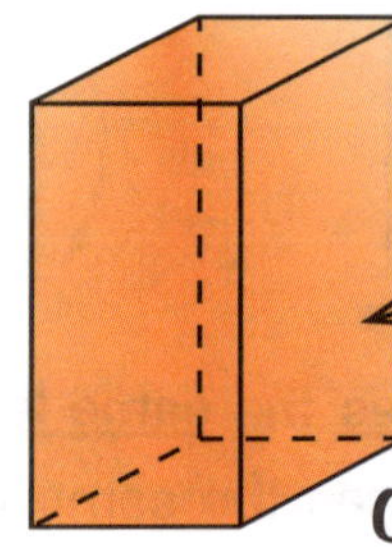

CUBOID

CYLINDER

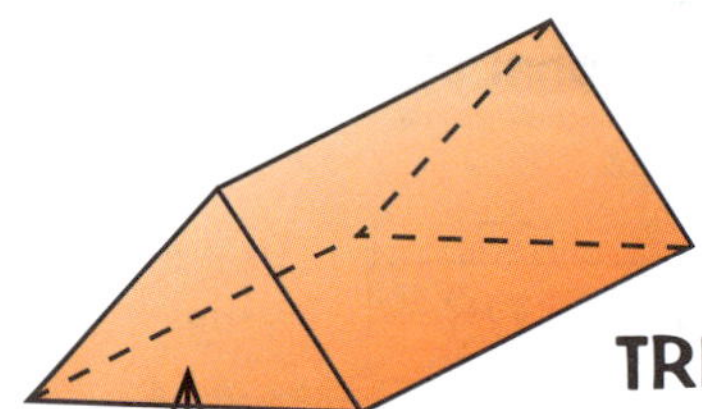

TRIANGULAR PRISM

Learn These Four Too:

These AREN'T PRISMS but you still need to know what pyramids, cones and spheres look like:

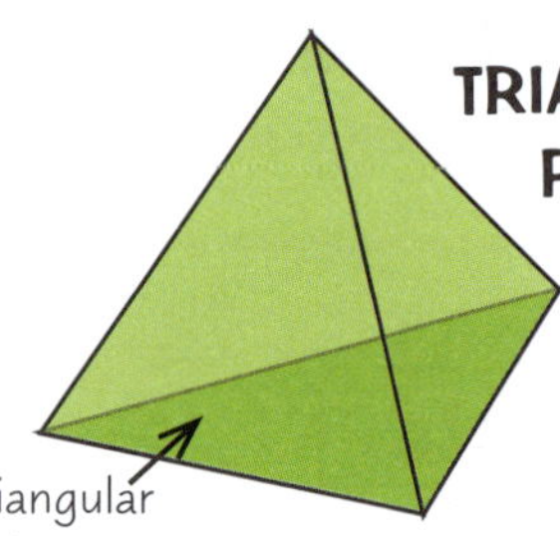

TRIANGULAR-BASED PYRAMID (or regular tetrahedron)

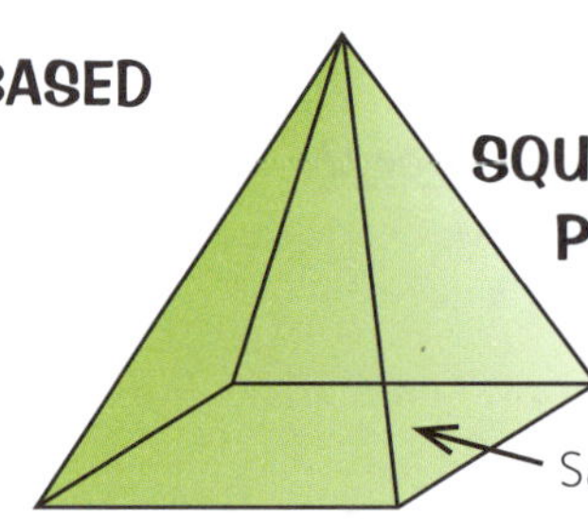

SQUARE-BASED PYRAMID

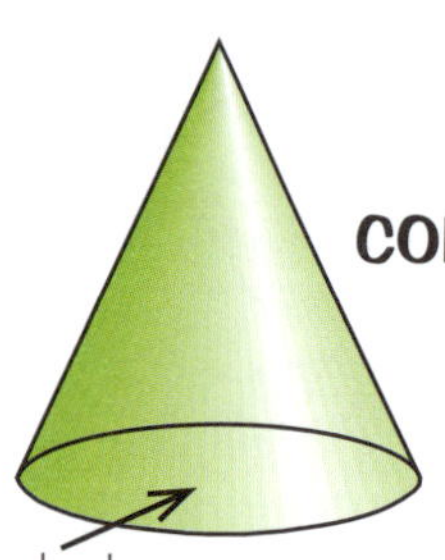

CONE

SPHERE (just a ball)

Well done — you've moved on to solids...

Deep breath in... and out... then learn the eight 3D shapes on this page.
Then cover up the page and see if you can name all eight different types of solid object.

Regular Polygons

A polygon is a many-sided shape. Regular polygons have some fancy features for you to learn.

A REGULAR polygon is one where ALL THE SIDES AND ANGLES are the SAME.

You Need to Know These Regular Polygons:

EQUILATERAL TRIANGLE

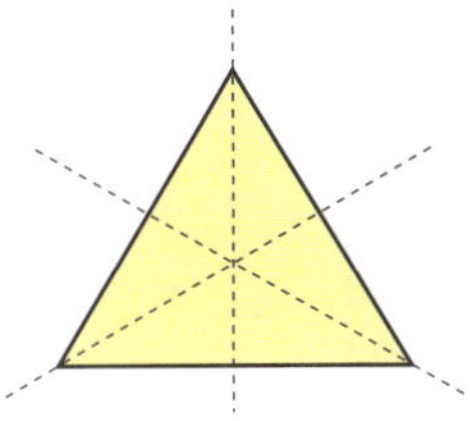

- 3 sides
- 3 lines of symmetry
- Rotational symmetry order 3

You should remember this from page 68.

SQUARE

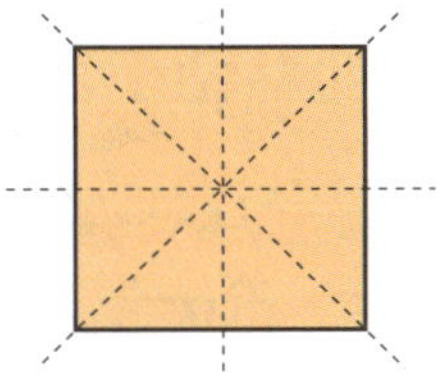

- 4 sides
- 4 lines of symmetry
- Rotational symmetry order 4

This was on page 69.

REGULAR PENTAGON

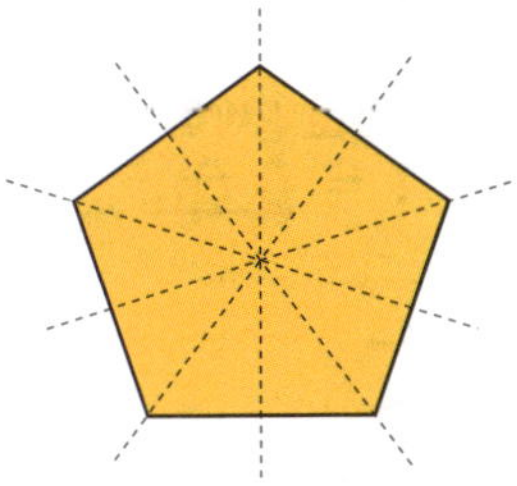

- 5 sides
- 5 lines of symmetry
- Rotational symmetry order 5

REGULAR HEXAGON

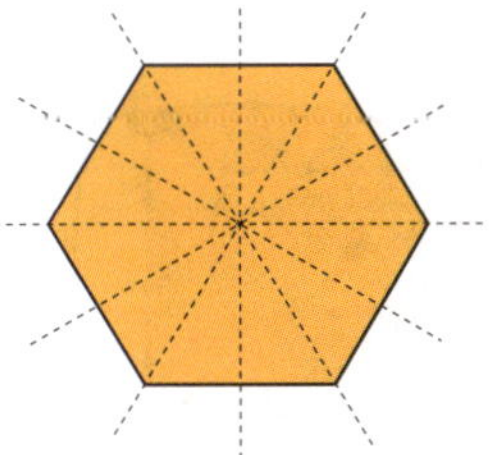

- 6 sides
- 6 lines of symmetry
- Rotational symmetry order 6

REGULAR HEPTAGON

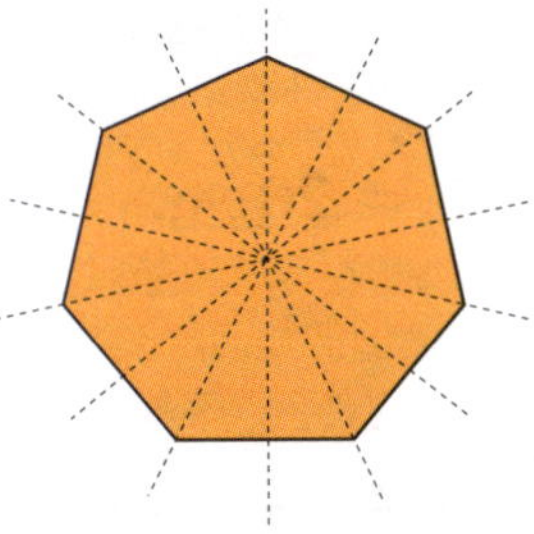

- 7 sides
- 7 lines of symmetry
- Rotational symmetry order 7

(A 50p piece is like a heptagon)

REGULAR OCTAGON

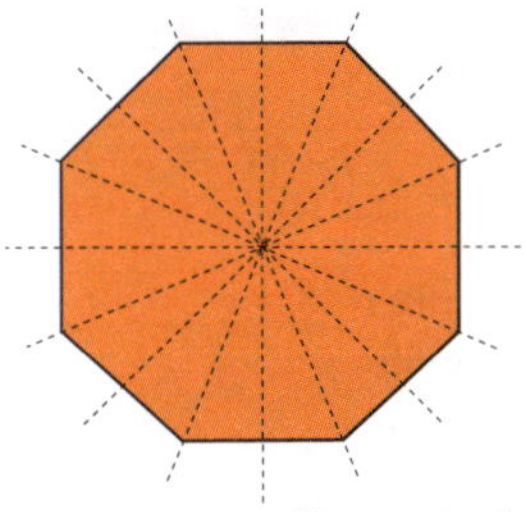

- 8 sides
- 8 lines of symmetry
- Rotational symmetry order 8

Remember — any 8-sided shape will be called an octagon, but a regular octagon must have all sides and angles the same.

EXCLUSIVE: Heptagon lottery winner says "I'm still just a regular guy"...

For regular polygons: number of sides = number of lines of symmetry = order of rotational symmetry.

1) What is a regular polygon?
2) Name the first six of them without looking at the page.

Perimeters

Perimeter is the distance all the way around the outside of a shape.
It helps if you can use the big blob method to work it out...

Perimeter is the Distance Around the Edge of a Shape

1) To find a PERIMETER, you ADD UP THE LENGTHS OF ALL THE SIDES.
2) To make sure you get all the sides, do this:

> 1) PUT A BIG BLOB AT ONE CORNER and then go around the shape.
> 2) WRITE DOWN THE LENGTH OF EVERY SIDE as you go along.
> 3) DON'T FORGET SIDES THAT SEEM TO HAVE NO LENGTH GIVEN — you must work them out first (see example).
> 4) Keep going until you get back to the BIG BLOB.

EXAMPLE: Find the perimeter of the shape below.

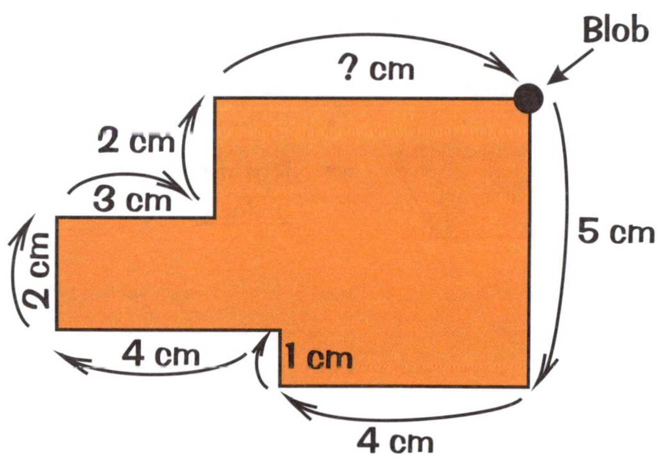

1) Check you know all the sides' lengths. One is missing here, so find this first.

2) Adding up the bottom lengths gives the width of the shape: 4 + 4 = 8 cm:

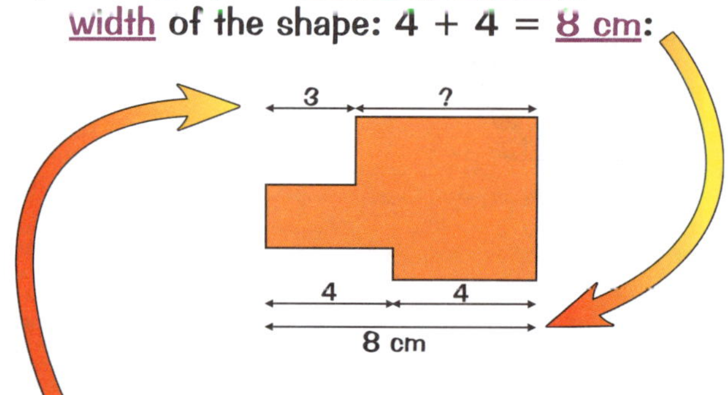

This must be the same across the top, so the missing length must be 8 – 3 = 5 cm.

3) So the perimeter must be:
5+4+1+4+2+3+2+5 = 26 cm.

You must choose yourself a blob and it must also choose you. It will then be yours for life.

RUN — DON'T WALK from... the BIG BLOB...

...no, don't do that really. You need to get friendly with your big blob, and always use him for finding the perimeter of shapes.
He should always be willing to help — if not, just feed him a calculator or two and he'll be happy in no time. He also quite likes cheese.

1) Turn over and write down what a perimeter is.
2) Find the perimeter of the shape shown here.

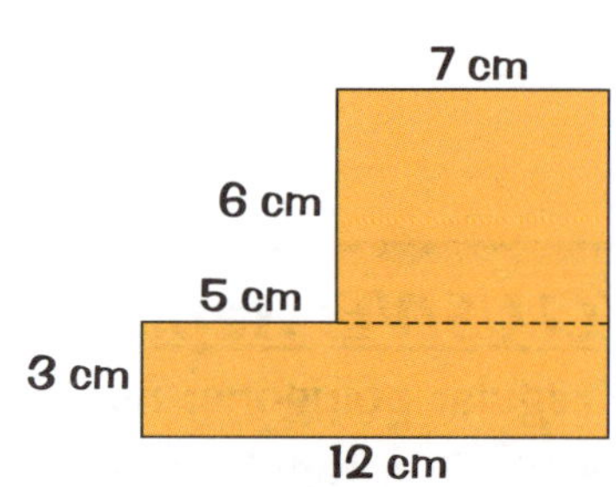

Areas

First things first — below are three formulas to work out the areas of shapes.
You need to learn these. Unless you want to wave goodbye to loads of exam marks...

You must LEARN these Formulas:

1) RECTANGLE

Area of RECTANGLE = length × width

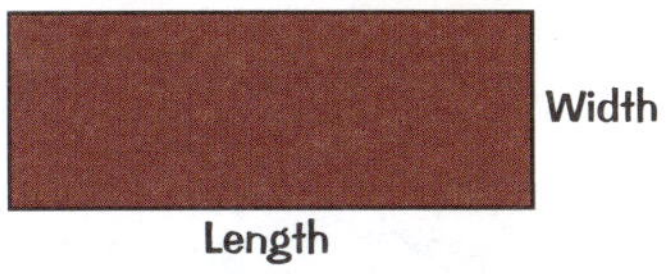

$A = l \times w$

area length width

Example: Area = length × width
Area = 12 m × 5 m
Area = 60 m^2.

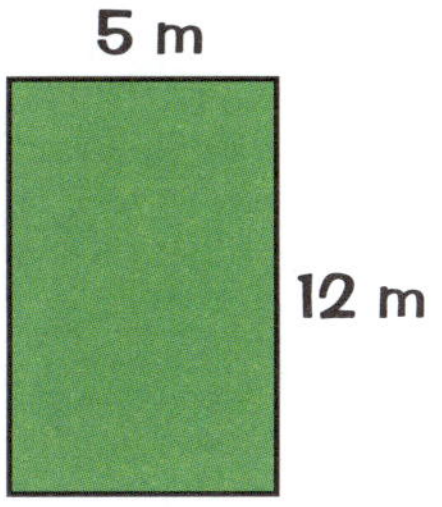

Units of area are always something squared — e.g. m^2 or cm^2.

2) TRIANGLE

Area of TRIANGLE = ½ × base × vertical height

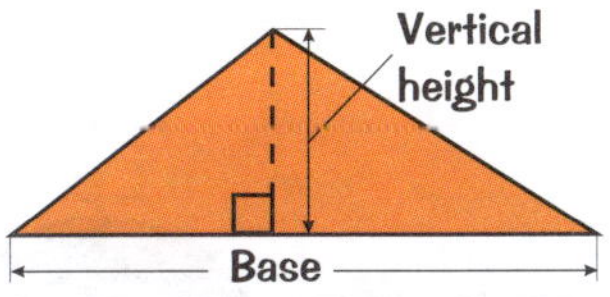

$A = \frac{1}{2} \times b \times h_v$

base vertical height

The height is always the vertical height, not the sloping height.

Example: Area = ½ × base × height
Area = ½ × 3 cm × 4 cm
Area = 6 cm^2.

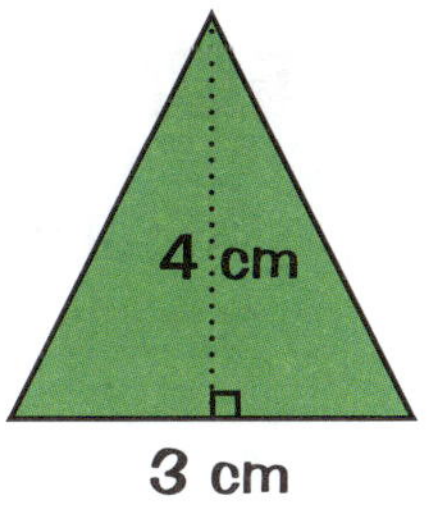

3) PARALLELOGRAM

Area of PARALLELOGRAM = base × vertical height

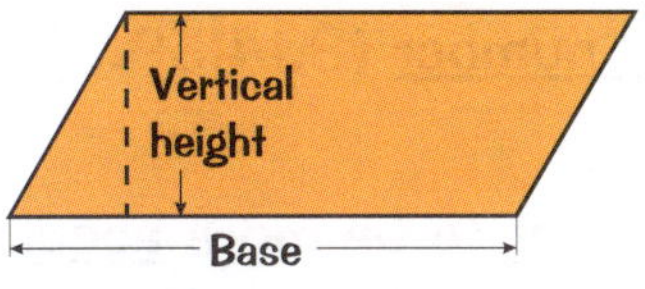

$A = b \times h_v$

Example: Area = base × height
Area = 5 cm × 3 cm
Area = 15 cm^2.

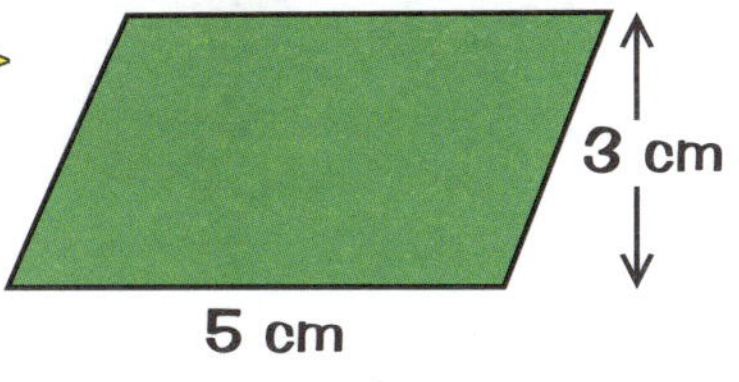

Again, use the vertical height, not the sloping height.

Make this your best area of maths...

Did I mention that you need to learn the formulas? Cover them up on the page, and have a go at these:

1) What is the area of a rectangle with length 8 cm and width 5 cm?
2) A triangle has a 10 cm base and a vertical height of 4 cm. What is the area of the triangle?

Circles

There are quite a few things about circles you need to know.
It's probably best to have a snack before starting this page. All the talk of pi can make you hungry.

Diameter and Radius

1) The DIAMETER goes right across the circle, through the centre (middle).

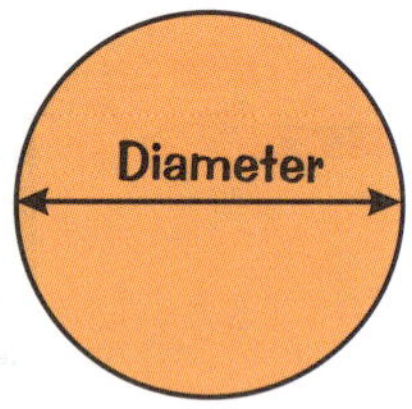

2) The RADIUS only goes halfway across, from the centre (middle).

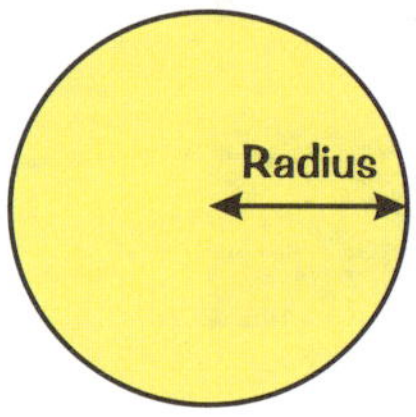

THE DIAMETER IS EXACTLY DOUBLE THE RADIUS

EXAMPLES: If the radius is 4 cm, the diameter is 4 cm × 2 = 8 cm.

If the diameter is 24 m, the radius is 24 m ÷ 2 = 12 m.

Circumference

1) The CIRCUMFERENCE is the distance round the outside of the circle.

2) The formula for circumference is:

Circumference = π × Diameter

π = 3.14159....
= about 3

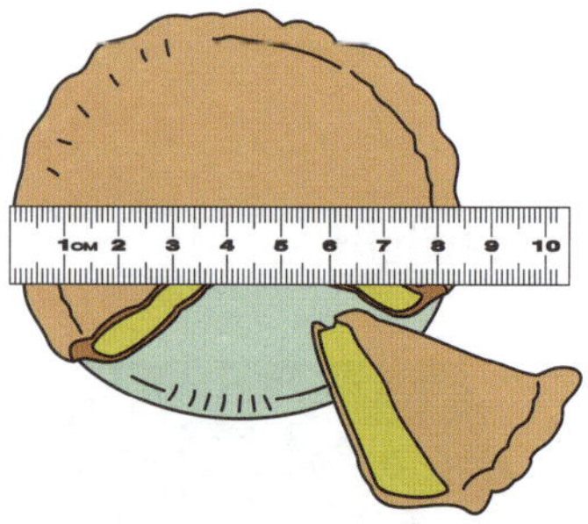

The symbol π (called "pi") is just an ordinary number (3.14159...).
It's usually rounded off to 3.14 or even just 3.
You can also use the π button on your calculator to be more accurate.

EXAMPLE: Find the circumference of a circle with radius 5 cm.

ANSWER: First find the diameter, which is double the radius: 5 × 2 = 10 cm.
Then use the formula: Circumference = π × Diameter = 3.14 × 10 = 31.4 cm.

Common mistake — a slice of pie is not called a wedgie...

Once again, learn it all, turn over and see what you can remember. If you can remember it all, reward yourself with a pie of your choice. Do I want a wedgie? Oh, well, if you're offering it's rude not to...

Volume

Learn the formulas on this page and you'll be able to find the volumes of loads of 3D shapes.

1) Cuboid (rectangular block)

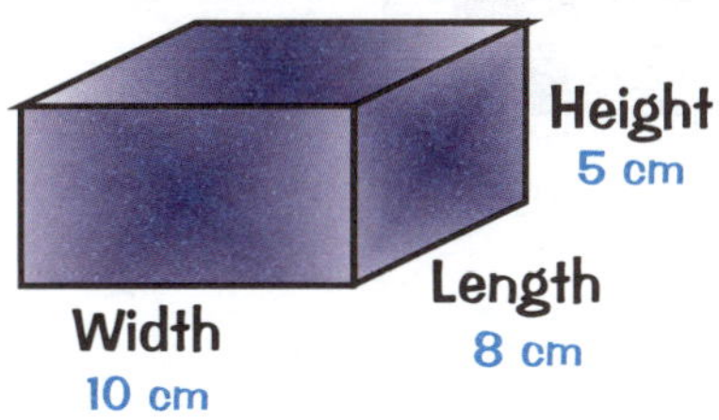

Volume of Cuboid = length × width × height

$$V = l \times w \times h$$

E.g. Volume = $8 \times 10 \times 5 = 400\ cm^3$.

Units of volume are always something *cubed* — e.g. m^3 or cm^3.

2) Prism

1) A PRISM is a solid (3D) shape which is the same shape all the way through — it has a CONSTANT AREA OF CROSS-SECTION (see page 70).

Triangular Prism

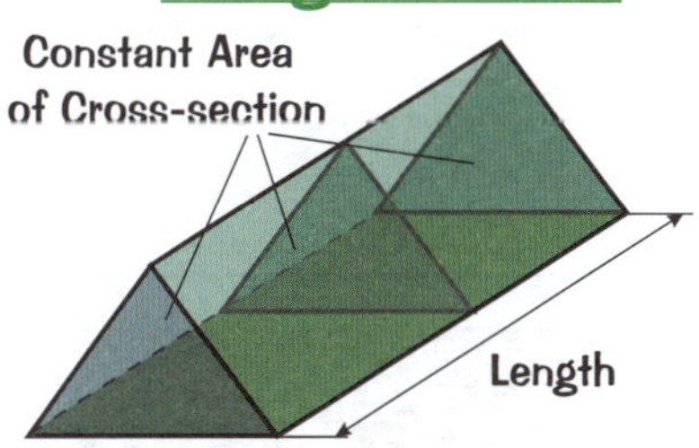

Circular Prism (or Cylinder)

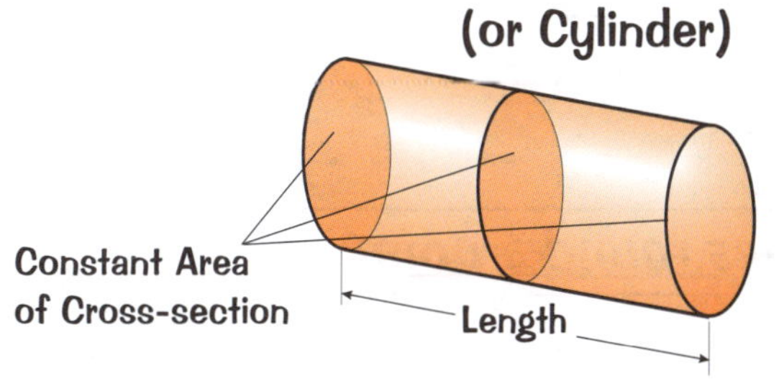

2) The formula for the volume of a prism is:

$$\text{Volume of prism} = \text{Cross-sectional Area} \times \text{length}$$

$$V = A \times l$$

EXAMPLE: Find the volume of this triangular prism.

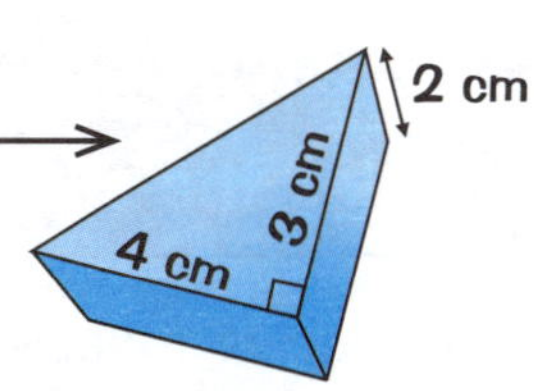

ANSWER: First find the area of the cross-section using the formula for the area of a triangle (see p.73).

Area = ½ × base × height = ½ × 4 × 3 = 6 cm^2.

Now use the formula for volume: $V = A \times l = 6 \times 2 = 12\ cm^3$.

Don't make it any more angry — it's already a cross-section...

Once you've learnt the formulas, just put the right numbers in and the answer is yours. All yours. Mwah-ha-ha-ha-haaaaaa. 1) Find the volume of this cuboid: (don't forget the units).

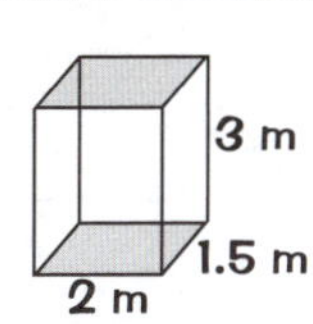

Five Angle Rules

Rules, rules, rules. You've got to love them. Or at least learn them.
Try these 5 simple rules for size:

1) Angles in a triangle

Add up to 180°.

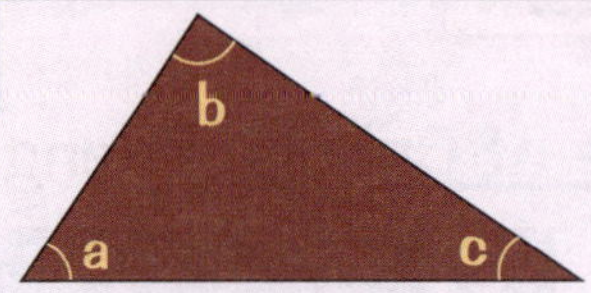

$a+b+c=180°$

2) Angles on a straight line

Add up to 180°.

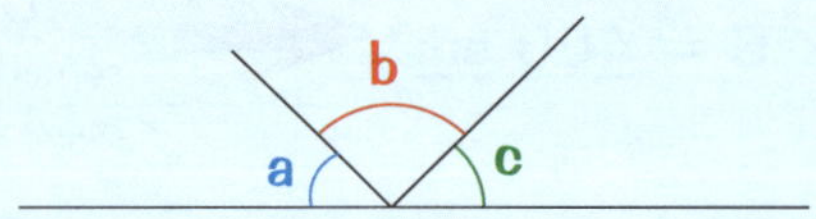

$a+b+c=180°$

3) Angles in a 4-sided shape

(a 'quadrilateral')
Add up to 360°.

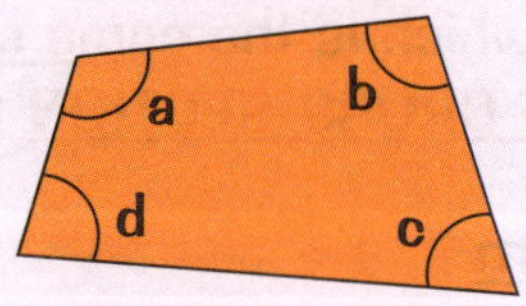

$a+b+c+d=360°$

4) Angles round a point

Add up to 360°.

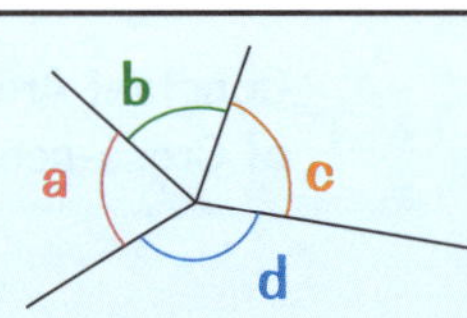

$a+b+c+d=360°$

5) Isosceles triangles

2 sides the same
2 angles the same

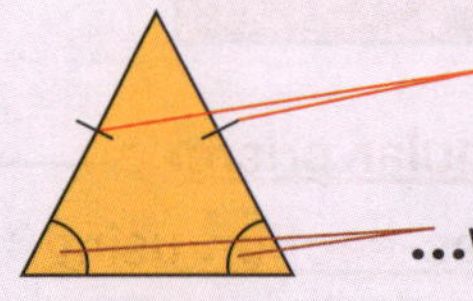

These lines mean the two sides are the same length...

...which means these angles are the same size.

In an isosceles triangle, YOU ONLY NEED TO KNOW ONE ANGLE to be able to find the other two.

a)

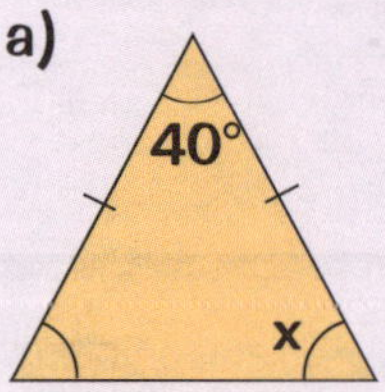

180° – 40° = 140° (see rule 1 above)
The two bottom angles are both the same and they must add up to 140°, so each one must be half of 140°. So x = 140° ÷ 2 = 70°.

b)

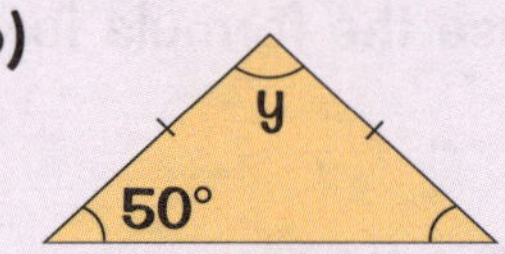

The two bottom angles must be the same, so 50° + 50° = 100°.
All the angles add up to 180° so y = 180° – 100° = 80°.

Parallel and Perpendicular Lines

Up next — parallel and perpendicular lines.
The names may sound scary, but if you learn the next two pages then you're off to a good start.

Angles and Lines

Perpendicular Lines

1) If two lines cross at 90° (right-angles) they're called perpendicular lines.

2) Mark on the right angle using a little square, like so:

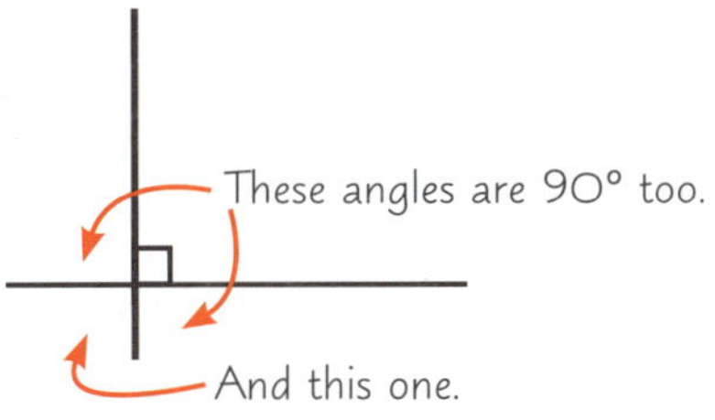

Parallel Lines

1) Parallel lines are lines that will never meet, no matter how far you stretch them out. They always stay the same distance apart.

2) Parallel lines are usually marked with little arrows, like this:

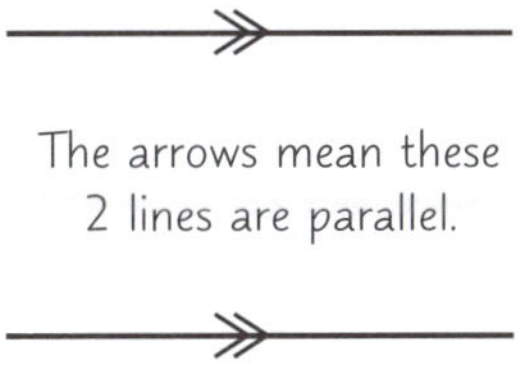

3) When a line cuts across 2 parallel lines, it makes two bunches of angles which are the same, as shown below:

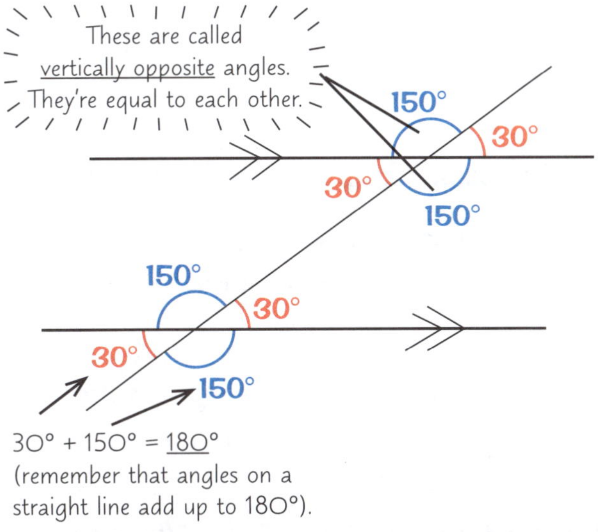

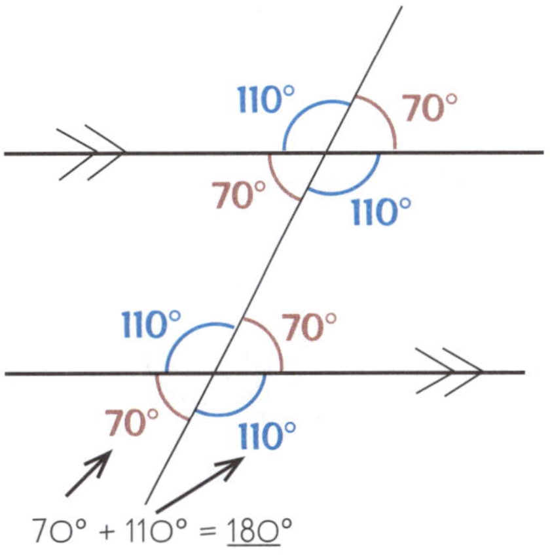

INSIDE THE BUNCHES OF ANGLES:

- there are only two different angles: A SMALLER ONE and A BIGGER ONE.
- the bigger angle and the smaller angle ALWAYS ADD UP TO 180°.
  (E.g. 30° and 150° or 70° and 110° in the examples above.)

Parallel and Perpendicular Lines

The hardest bit about angles around parallel lines is spotting them in the first place.
Once you've done that, you can have fun working out what the angles are. Well, I say 'fun'...

Angles Between Parallel Lines

1) When you have a line crossing a pair of parallel lines, loads of the angles are either

THE SAME AS EACH OTHER OR **ADD TOGETHER TO MAKE 180°**

2) These 'Z', 'F', 'C' and 'U' shapes will tell you which angles do what:

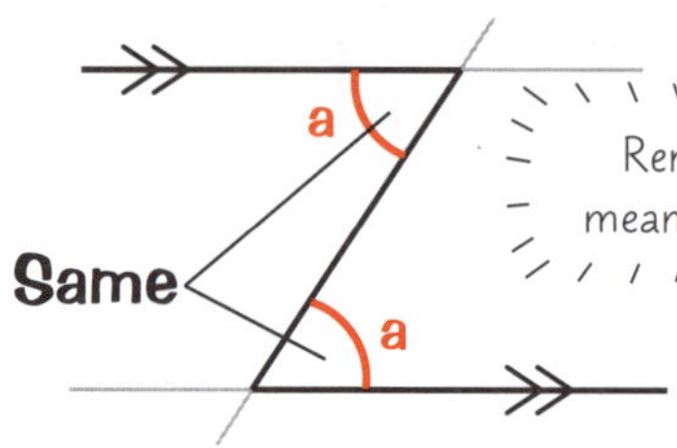

Remember, the arrows mean they're parallel lines.

In a Z-shape they're called ALTERNATE ANGLES

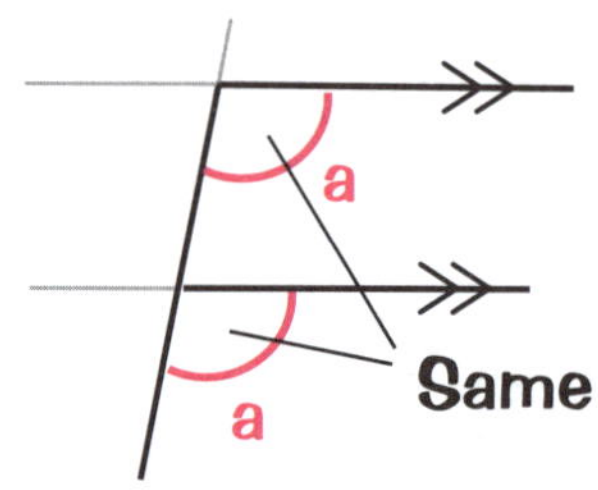

In an F-shape they're called CORRESPONDING ANGLES

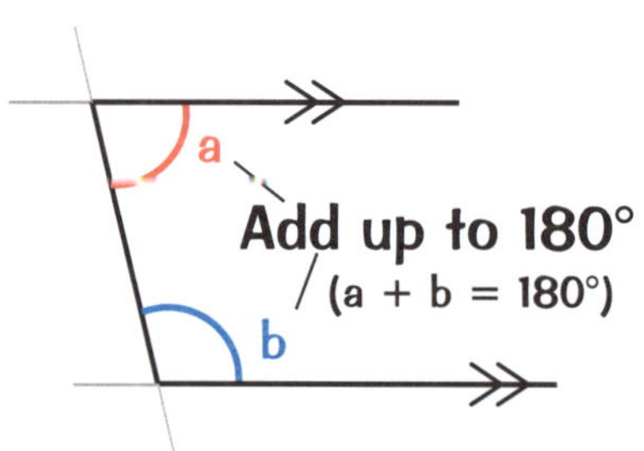

If they add up to 180°, like in the C and U shapes they're called SUPPLEMENTARY ANGLES

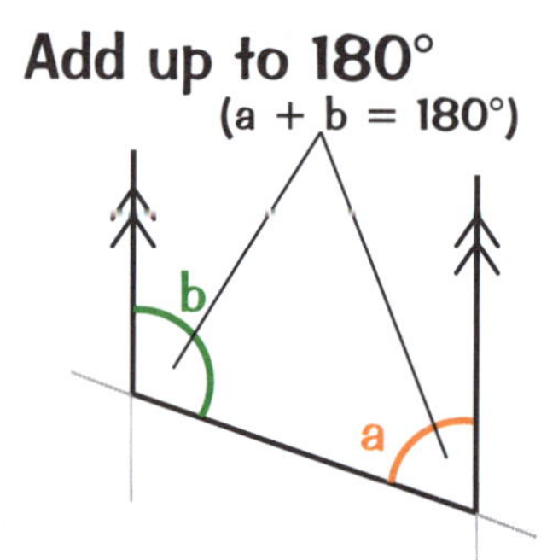

EXAMPLE: Find the size of angles A, B and C in the diagram below:

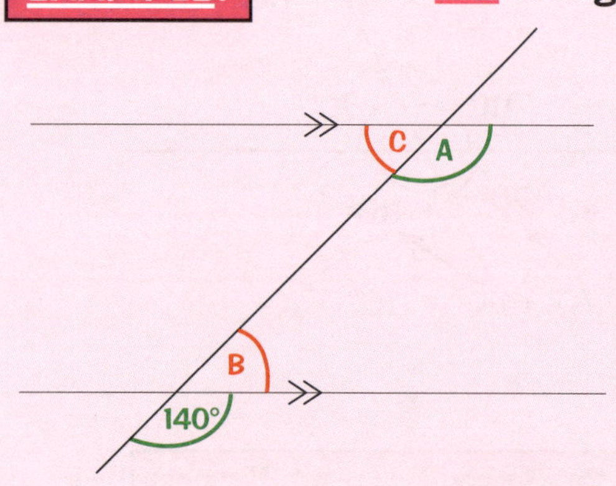

1) Angle A is in an 'F' shape (corresponding) with the 140° angle, so this means it's THE SAME: A = 140°.

2) Angle B is in a 'C' shape (supplementary) with angle A (140°) so they ADD TO MAKE 180°: B = 180° – 140° = 40°.

3) Angle 'C' is in a 'Z' shape (alternate) with angle B (40°) so this means it's THE SAME: C = 40°.

Parallel line spotting — not the coolest of hobbies...

Spotting parallel lines is really, really important, so always have a good look for them. You don't want to miss them. Have a practice with this:

1) The diagram shown here has one angle given as 60°. Find all the other 7 angles.

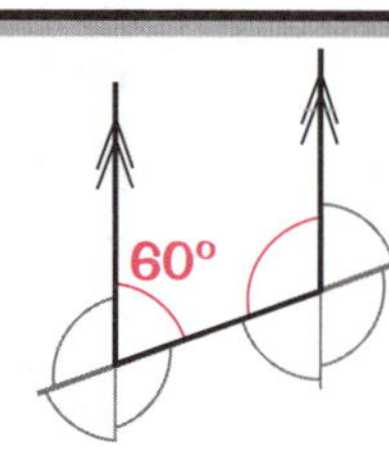

Revision Test for Unit 3 — 1

1) Sharon is making some birthday cards. She wants to fold each card along a line of symmetry, so it folds exactly together.
Draw all the lines of symmetry for each of the card designs.
a) 
b) 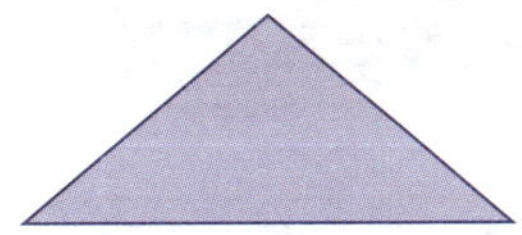
c) 

2) Give the order of rotational symmetry for each of the designs above.

3) The shape on the right is an isosceles triangle.
a) What is the length of side A?
b) What's special about angles B and C?

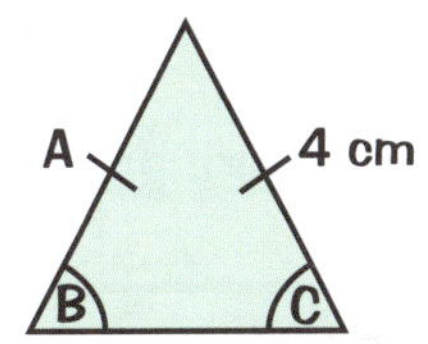

4) What 4-sided shape has all its sides the same length AND only 2 lines of symmetry?

5) Sketch these four shapes, and say which are prisms:
a) Triangular Prism b) Cone c) Cylinder d) Sphere

6) Write down everything you know about regular octagons.

7) Alison wants to put a fence around the whole perimeter of her garden, shown below.
a) Work out the missing length on the plan of the garden.
b) How many metres of fencing should Alison buy?

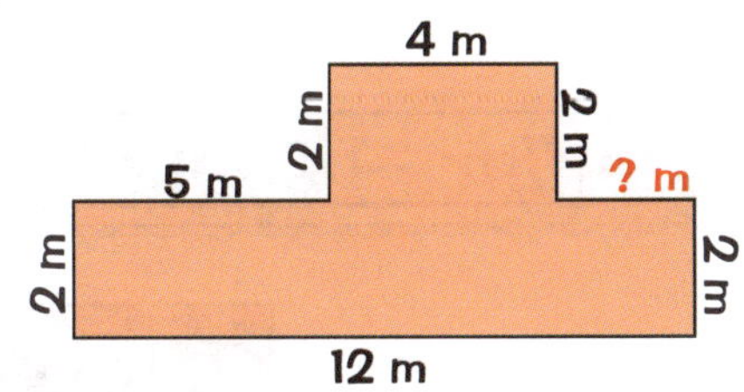

8) Clive is re-carpeting his lounge, which is rectangular.
The room is 12 m long and 7 m wide.
What area of carpet does he need?

9) Find the area of:
a) a triangle with base 4 cm and vertical height 9 cm.
b) a parallelogram with base 12 cm and vertical height 3 cm.

10) A plate has a radius of 6 cm. Find its circumference.

11) A prism has a cross-sectional area of 55 cm^2, and a length of 100 cm.
Find its volume (don't forget the units).

12) Work out the missing angle inside the quadrilateral on the right.

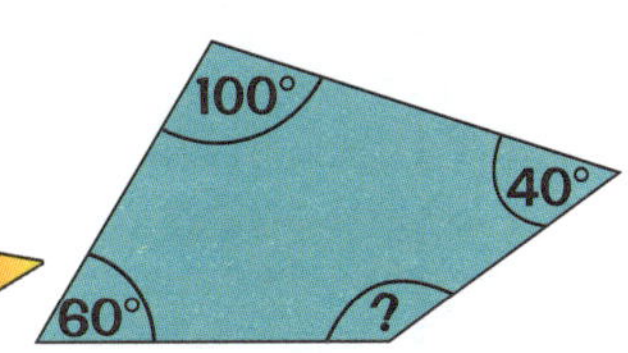

Use some of the 'five angle rules' to do Q12 and Q13.

13) Work out angles X and Y in this diagram:

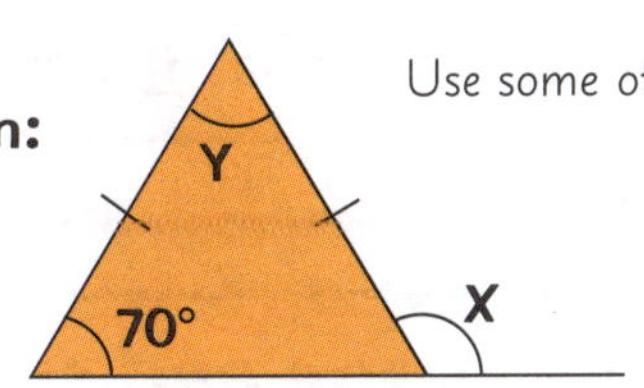

14) a) What is the size of angle b in the diagram on the right?
b) What is the special name given to a pair of angles like a and b?

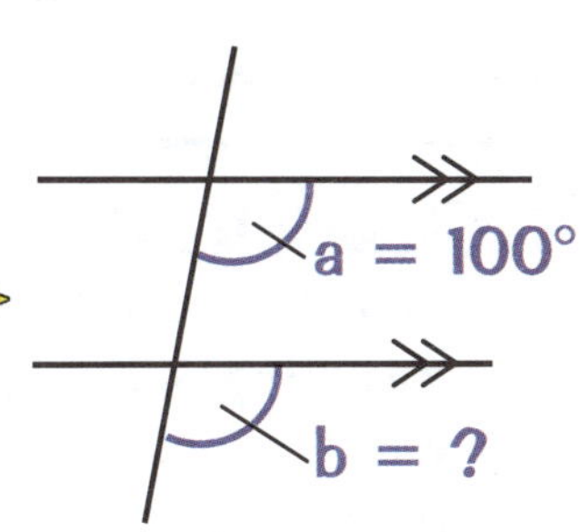

Congruence and Similarity

Shapes can be congruent or similar. And I bet you really want to know what that means. Well, lucky you — I've written a page all about it.

Congruent — Same Shape, Same Size

If two shapes are CONGRUENT, they are simply THE SAME — the SAME SIZE and the SAME SHAPE.

E.g. The shapes below are all congruent. They've just been drawn in different positions.

CONGRUENT: Same size, same shape.
Note — you can have mirror images.

Similar — Same Shape, Different Size

If two shapes are SIMILAR they are exactly the SAME SHAPE but DIFFERENT SIZES.

Two similar shapes can be seen as an 'enlargement'... see page 82.

SIMILAR: Same shape, different size.

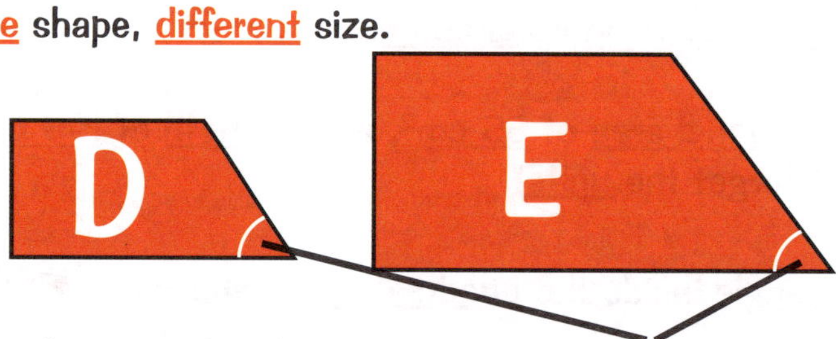

When you have similar shapes the angles are always the same.

Pizza and a frisbee — same shape and size but don't get them confused...

Know what congruent and similar mean — it's important you don't get them mixed up.

1) a) Which of these four shapes are similar? i)  ii)  iii)  iv) 
   b) Which are congruent?

The Four Transformations — Translation

Shapes can be transformed (changed) by changing their position or size, spinning or reflecting them. There are four types of transformation — let's kick things off with a look at translation.

Translation means Sliding

1) A translation is just a SLIDE.
   The shape just slides to another place.
2) You have to say how far along and how far up or down the shape has moved.
3) You'll often be given shapes on a grid like the one below.
4) You have to say how many squares along and how many up or down a shape has moved.

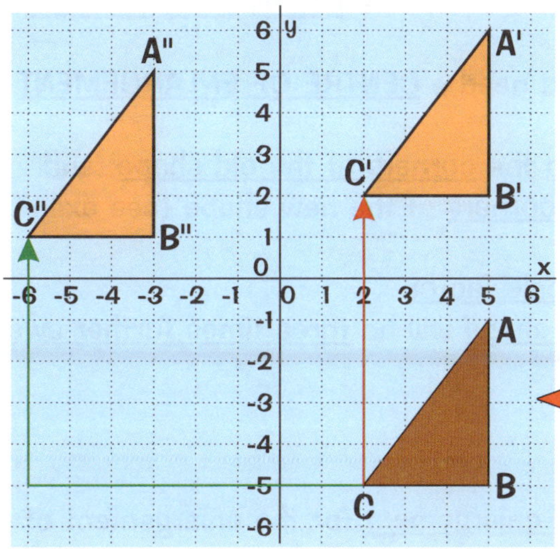

EXAMPLES:
ABC to A'B'C' is a translation of 7 up.
ABC to A''B''C'' is a translation of 8 left and 6 up.

It helps if you just look at how one corner of the shape has moved. The arrows show how corner C has moved 7 squares up for the first translation, and 8 squares left and 6 up for the second one.

Give Your Answer in the Right Form

1) To get marks in the exam, you need to give translations in what's known as 'vector form'.
2) This looks like a pair of coordinates (see page 59) 'standing up':

The top number 'x' is the number of spaces right.
The bottom number 'y' is the number of spaces up.

$$\begin{pmatrix} x \rightarrow \\ \uparrow y \end{pmatrix}$$

If the shape has moved left or down, just use negative numbers.

3) For example, '7 up' is just $\begin{pmatrix} 0 \\ 7 \end{pmatrix}$, because there's no movement left or right.
4) A translation of 8 left and 6 up is written: $\begin{pmatrix} -8 \\ 6 \end{pmatrix}$.

Don't get lost in translation...

When you're trying to see how far up and along a shape has moved, just focus on one of the corners to see where its 'matching' corner has moved to. Same goes if you're trying to draw a translated shape. Just move each point on the shape one at a time, then join the dots to finish the new shape.

The Four Transformations — Enlargement

Enlargement is just making something B I G G E R.

Shapes Are Enlarged By a Scale Factor

To describe an enlargement you must know 2 things:

1) The SCALE FACTOR
2) The CENTRE OF ENLARGEMENT

1) The SCALE FACTOR is how many times bigger the new shape is than the old shape.
2) E.g. a scale factor of 3 makes it three times as big — each side trebles (×3) in length.
3) For enlargements on a grid (like the one below) you need a CENTRE OF ENLARGEMENT too.
4) If you draw lines from the centre of enlargement to the corners of the old shape, and stretch them out, they should touch the matching corners of the new shape (see example).
5) The length of the stretched lines depends on the scale factor. E.g. for a scale factor of 3, each corner of the big shape will be three times further away from the centre of enlargement as the small shape.

Example: Find the scale factor and centre of enlargement for the enlargement of A to B.

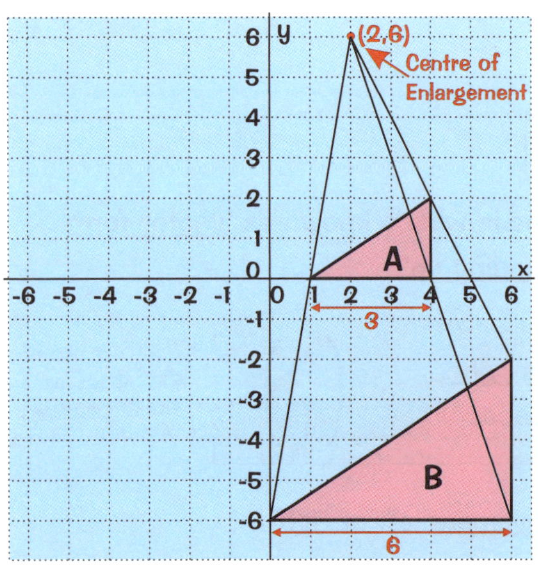

With enlargement, the angles of the two shapes are the same — they're similar (see p.80). The size and position of the shapes are different.

1) SCALE FACTOR:

Compare side lengths of the two shapes.

A has a base of 3, and B has a base of 6.

This means B is twice as big as A (6 ÷ 3 = 2) so the scale factor is 2.

2) CENTRE OF ENLARGEMENT:

Join up the corners of B to the matching corners of A, and stretch out the lines until they meet.

The point where they meet is the centre of enlargement — here it's at (2,6).

A to B is an enlargement of scale factor 2, centre (2,6).

Go on — supersize me...

It's easy to spot an enlargement — it's the only one of the four transformations that changes the size of a shape. You've got to know how to find the scale factor and centre of enlargement too though.

The Four Transformations — Rotation

Two down, two to go... A rotation turns a shape around.

You Need to Know 3 Things For Rotation

As well as spotting that a shape has been rotated, you need to give these 3 details:

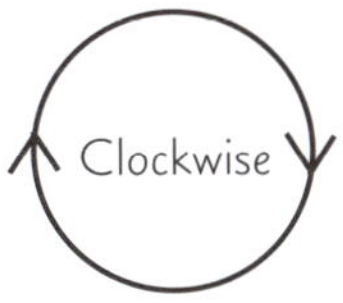

1) The ANGLE it's been turned by.
2) The DIRECTION of the turn (Clockwise or Anticlockwise).
3) The CENTRE OF ROTATION — the point it's been turned 'about'.

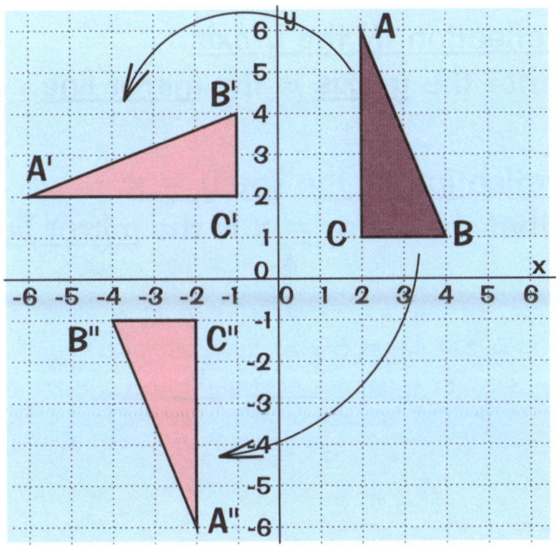

EXAMPLES:

ABC to A'B'C' is a rotation of:
90°, anticlockwise, ABOUT the origin (0,0).

ABC to A''B''C'' is a rotation of:
half a turn (180°), clockwise, ABOUT the origin (0,0).
(For half-turns, it doesn't actually matter if you go clockwise or anticlockwise.)

Use Tracing Paper To Check

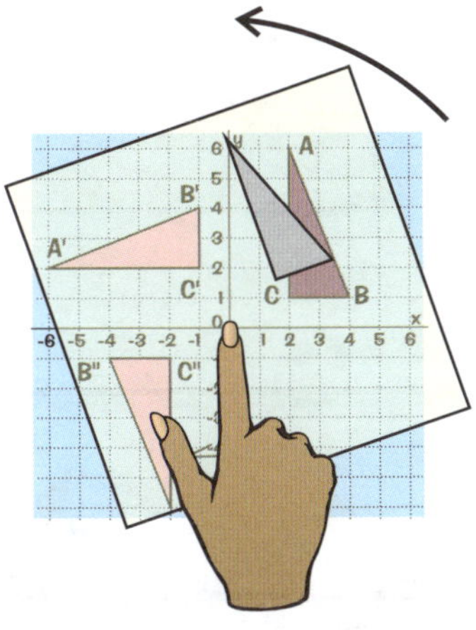

Tracing paper can help with rotations:

1) Trace around the old shape.

2) Hold the tracing paper at the centre of rotation (just put your finger there).

3) Spin the tracing paper round, by the angle and direction given, and check that the tracing lines up with the new shape.

This page makes me dizzy...

Rotations can sometimes be trickier to spot than the other three transformations. So, if it doesn't look like any of the others, chances are it's a rotation. Don't forget to give all three details.

The Four Transformations — Reflection

Last one now... A reflection is just a mirror image. You have to say where the mirror is though.

Give The Mirror Line For Reflections

1) If a shape has been REFLECTED, you only need to say where the MIRROR LINE is.
2) Each corner of the new shape will be the SAME DISTANCE AWAY from the mirror line as the matching corner of the old shape.

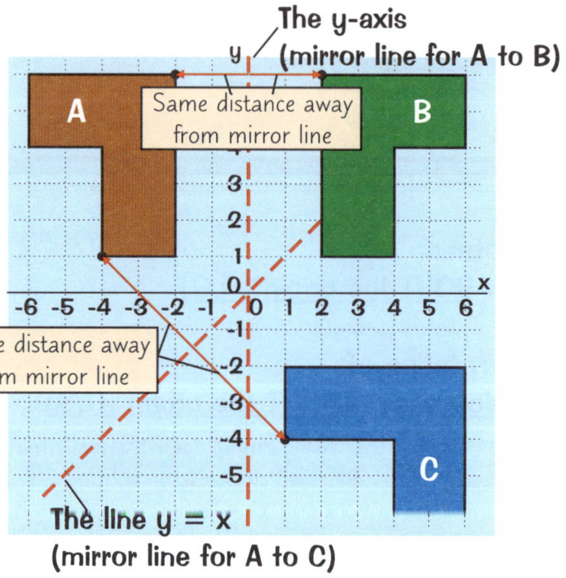

EXAMPLES:

A to B is a reflection IN the y-axis.
This means that the y-axis is the mirror line.

A to C is a reflection IN the line $y = x$.
This means that the line $y = x$ is the mirror line.

See pages 60-61 for a reminder of equations of straight lines.

Tracing Paper Helps With Reflections

Tracing paper sure is useful stuff...

1) Trace around the old shape and along the mirror line.
2) Flip the tracing paper over and line up the mirror lines.
3) The drawing of the old shape on the tracing paper should line up with the new shape.

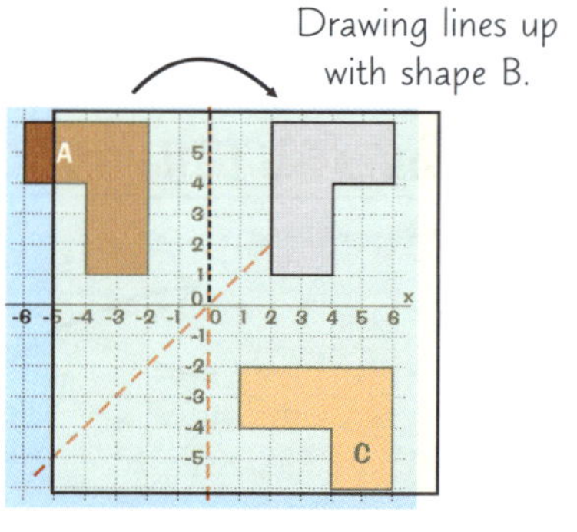

Time to reflect on the last few pages...

That's all four transformations done. Hurrah. Before you move on:
LEARN the names of the four transformations and the details for each.
Then, when you think you know it, turn over and see what you've learnt.
Finally, do a dance to celebrate. Any dance will do.

1) Describe fully these 4 transformations:

A to B, B to C, C to A, A to D.

Use tracing paper to help you.

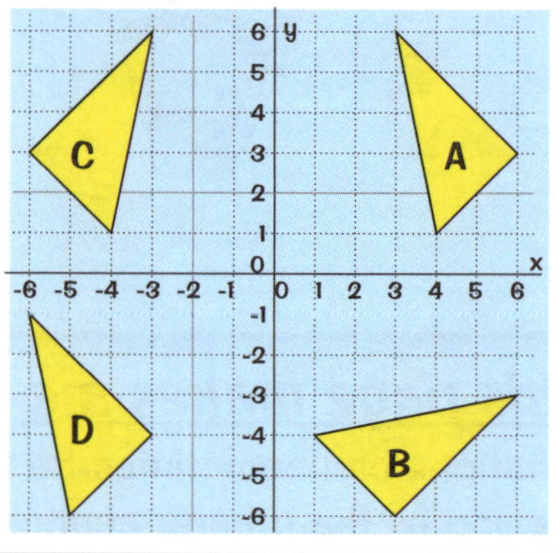

Speed

Speed is how fast something's moving. You need to know the speed formula and how to use it. Luckily there's a formula triangle on hand to help.

Speed = Distance ÷ Time

1) To work out how fast something's going, you need to know the time taken to go a certain distance.
2) Then use the formula:

Speed = Distance ÷ Time

EXAMPLE: If I take 2 hours to walk 8 miles, what is my speed?
ANSWER: Speed = distance ÷ time = 8 miles ÷ 2 hours = 4 miles per hour (mph).

Use the Triangle for Distance and Time

1) You might be given the speed of something and be asked to find:
   a) the distance it travels in a certain time OR b) the time it takes to go a certain distance.
2) These problems are loads easier with this formula triangle.
3) To use the triangle, just cover up the letter of the thing you're after, then what's left is the formula you need.
4) For example, to get the formula for 'distance', cover up the 'D'. This leaves you with 'S × T', so the formula is D = S × T (Distance = Speed × Time).
5) You need to LEARN where the letters go in this triangle — they won't give it to you in the exam.

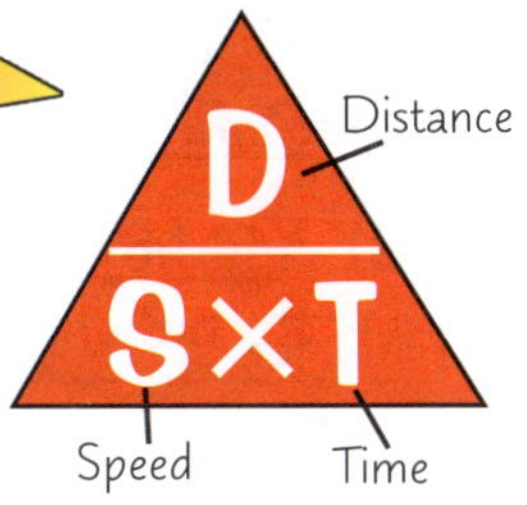

EXAMPLE: A car travels 90 miles at 30 miles per hour. How long does it take?

ANSWER: We want to find the TIME, so cover up T in the triangle which leaves $\frac{D}{S}$.
So T = D ÷ S
Time = Distance ÷ speed = 90 ÷ 30 = 3 hours

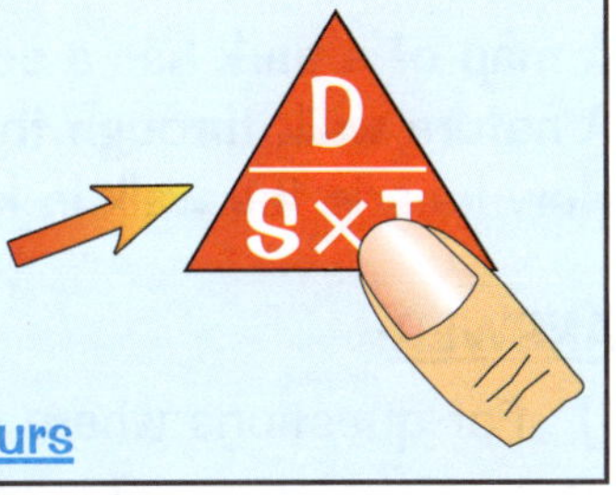

Formula triangles — it's all a big cover up...

Formula triangles are the most useful thing ever. They make remembering things like the speed formula much easier. Learn the whole page, cover it up, and write down the formula triangle for speed.

Maps and Map Scales

The most usual map scale is "1 cm = so many km". This just tells you how many km in real life it is for 1 cm measured on the actual map. This is really useful stuff to learn if you're planning a journey, or taking a maths exam any time soon...

Converting "cm on the Map" into "Real km"

EXAMPLE 1:

This map shows the original M6 Motorway built by the Romans in AD120.

The scale of the map is 1 cm to 8 km.

Work out the length of the section of M6 between Wigan and Preston.

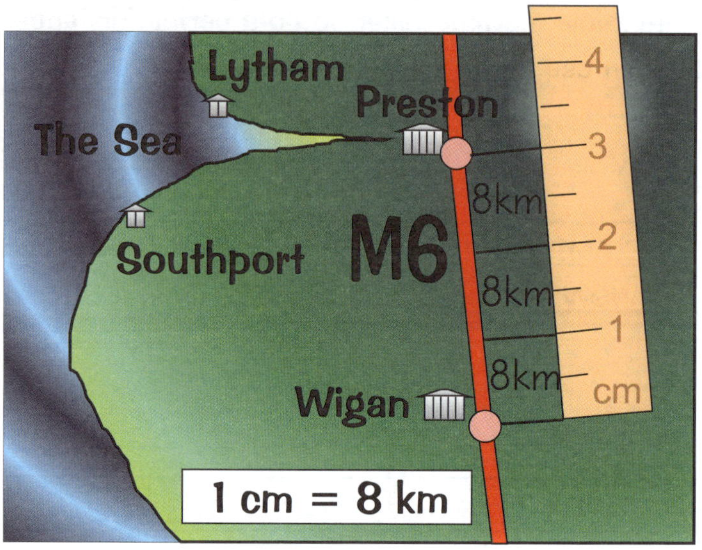

ANSWER: as shown on the map:

1) Put your ruler against the bit you're finding the length of.
Make sure the zero on the ruler is lined up with the starting place (in this case, Wigan).
2) Mark off each whole cm and write next to each one the distance in km.
3) Add up all the km you just marked.
So between Wigan and Preston: 8 km + 8 km + 8 km = 24 km.

EXAMPLE 2:

A map of a park has a scale of 1 cm to 0.1 km.
A nature walk through the park measures 7 cm on the map.
How long is the walk in km?

ANSWER:

1) For questions where you don't have a map, you won't be able to put your ruler on it.
2) Instead, draw a line 7 cm long and then mark off the km on it using your ruler just the same.

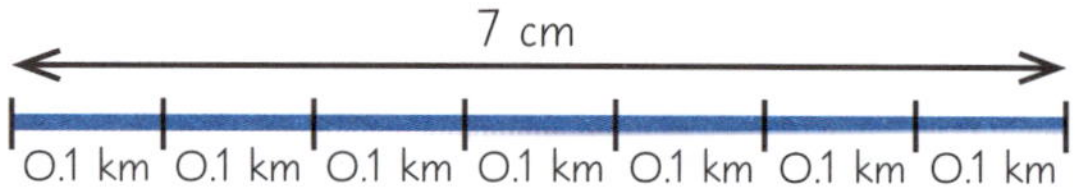

3) So the distance is:
0.1 + 0.1 + 0.1 + 0.1 + 0.1 + 0.1 + 0.1
= 7 × 0.1 = 0.7 km.

Maps and Map Scales

You also need to know how to work out sizes on a map or scale drawing using the 'real life' size. This is handy if you want to draw something to scale.

Converting "Real km" into "cm on the Map"

EXAMPLE: A map is drawn on a scale of 1 cm to 2 km.
If a road is 12 km long in real life, how long will it be in cm on the map?

ANSWER:

1) Start by drawing the road as a straight line:
2) Mark off each cm and fill in how many km it is for each one:

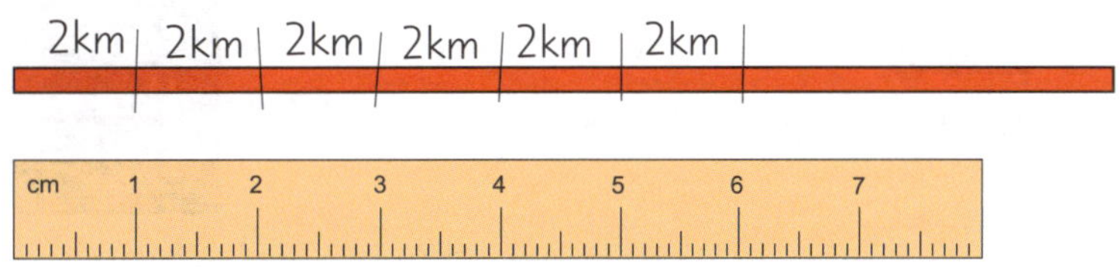

3) Keep going until the km add up to the full distance. (12 km in this case.)
4) Then just count how many cms long your line is — in this case it's 6 cm.

It Works For Other Scales Too

EXAMPLE: Larry wants to draw a picture of his robot, Barry, to a scale of 1 cm to 20 cm. How tall will Barry be on the drawing if he is 80 cm tall in real life?

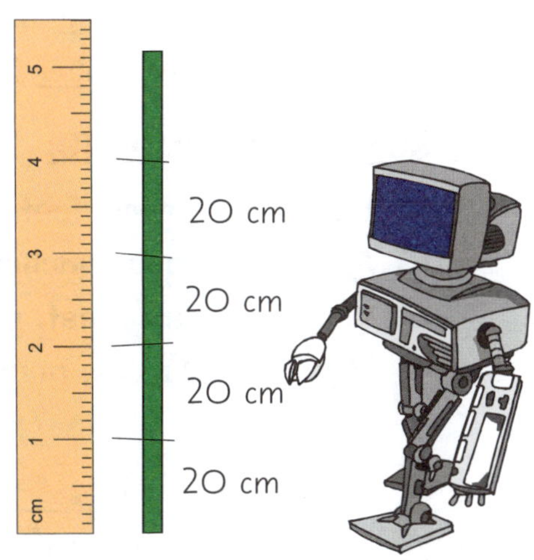

ANSWER:

1) Draw the height as a straight line.
2) Mark off each cm and fill in how many 'real life' cm it is.
3) Keep going until you get the full height. (80 cm.)
4) Count how many cms long your line is — in this case it's 4 cm.

What's the king of the pencil case?

The ruler... Sorry... Right, have a go at these:

1) Work out the length in metres of the runway shown here: →
2) How many cm on the map would a 600 m runway be? (HINT: use the scale shown on the map).

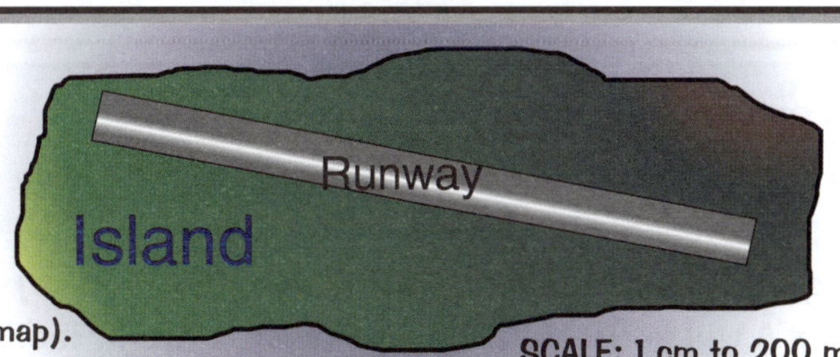

Metric and Imperial Units

Learning this stuff means more than just exam marks.
It can also help you out with many a dog-related problem*.

Metric Units

You can spot metric units because they often start with things like 'milli' and 'kilo'.
To change between them you have to times or divide by 10, 100, 1000... etc. as shown below.

SOME METRIC UNITS:

1) Length mm, cm, m, km
2) Area mm^2, cm^2, m^2, km^2
3) Volume mm^3, cm^3, m^3, litres, ml
4) Mass g, kg, tonnes

MEMORISE THESE KEY FACTS:

1 cm = 10 mm	1 tonne = 1000 kg
1 m = 100 cm	1 litre = 1000 ml
1 km = 1000 m	1 litre = 1000 cm^3
1 kg = 1000 g	1 cm^3 = 1 ml

EXAMPLE: My brother is 180 cm tall. How tall is he in a) mm, and b) m?

a) 1 cm = 10 mm, so 180 cm must be 180 × 10 = 1800 mm.
b) 100 cm = 1 m, so 180 cm must be 180 ÷ 100 = 1.80 m.

There's more on how to change between units on p.90, so don't panic if you don't quite get it yet.

Imperial Units

Imperial units are 'old style' units. We still use them though (e.g. giving heights in feet and inches).
You don't need to remember these conversions in the exam, but you need to be able to use them.

SOME IMPERIAL UNITS:

1) Length Inches, feet, yards, miles
2) Area Square inches, square miles
3) Volume Cubic feet, gallons, pints
4) Mass Ounces, pounds, stones, tons

IMPERIAL UNIT CONVERSIONS:

1 Foot = 12 Inches
1 Yard = 3 Feet
1 Gallon = 8 Pints
1 Stone = 14 Pounds (lbs)
1 Pound = 16 Ounces (oz)

EXAMPLE: *My dog weighs 2 stones. How many pounds is this?
1 stone = 14 lbs, so 2 stones must be 2 × 14 = 28 lbs.

Imperial units — they're mint...

Learn the bits in the blue box, then cover the page and try to scribble them all down.

1) a) How many cm is 2 metres? b) How many mm is 65 cm?
2) a) How many kg is 2000 g? b) How many litres is 3000 cm^3?
3) A rod is 48 inches long. What is this in feet?

Metric and Imperial Units

Sometimes you need to swap between metric and imperial units.
We only have approximate (rough) conversions between the two, but that's all you need really.

Metric-Imperial Conversions

LEARN THESE FOUR:

Approximate Conversions

1 kg = 2.2 pounds (lbs)

1 gallon = 4.5 litres

1 inch = 2.5 cm

1 mile = 1.6 km
(or 5 miles = 8 km)

Now see how to use them with these puppy-based examples:

Example 1: "My puppy weighs 5 kg. What is this in pounds (lbs)?"

1) 1 kg is about 2.2 lbs (from the box above).
2) So 5 kg is about 5 × 2.2 = 11 lbs.

Example 2: "I walk my puppy 2 miles every day. How far is this in kilometres?"

1) 1 mile is about 1.6 km.
2) So 2 miles is about 2 × 1.6 = 3.2 km.

Example 3: "My puppy likes special doggy ice cream as a treat. He gets through 3 gallons in a week. How much is this in litres?"

1) 1 gallon is about 4.5 litres.
2) So 3 gallons is about 3 × 4.5 = 13.5 litres.

This page has left me feeling a bit rough...

...Or maybe I mixed up my tub of vanilla with the "Chicken and Liver" flavour in the freezer. Yuck.
Now, learn the four conversions in the red box, then cover them up and see how many you remember.

Conversion Factors

A conversion factor is just a number that tells you how many times bigger or smaller one thing is compared to another. For example, a kilogram (kg) is 1000 times bigger than a gram (g), so the conversion factor is 1000. You can use them to change between different units.

Method

1) Find the CONVERSION FACTOR.
2) Multiply AND divide by the conversion factor.
3) Choose the COMMON SENSE ANSWER.
(This is just the answer that seems most likely).

Example 1:

"A Giant Sea-slug called Kevin was washed up near Grange-Over-Sands. He was 18.6 m in length. How long is this in cm?"

See page 88 for the conversion factors.

Step 1) Find the CONVERSION FACTOR
In this question the Conversion Factor = 100
(because 1 m = 100 cm)

Step 2) MULTIPLY AND DIVIDE by the conversion factor:
18.6 m × 100 = 1860 cm (seems okay)
18.6 m ÷ 100 = 0.186 cm (way too small)

Step 3) Choose the COMMON SENSE answer:
The answer is 18.6 m = 1860 cm

Example 2:

"Lisa's garden pond holds 200 pints of water.
How much is this in gallons, if 1 gallon is 8 pints?"

Step 1) Find the CONVERSION FACTOR
Conversion Factor = 8 (because 1 gallon = 8 pints)

Step 2) MULTIPLY AND DIVIDE by the conversion factor:
200 pints × 8 = 1600 gallons
200 pints ÷ 8 = 25 gallons

Step 3) Choose the COMMON SENSE answer:
A gallon must be bigger than a pint if there are 8 pints in a gallon.
So there must be fewer gallons than pints in the pond.
The answer must be 200 pints = 25 gallons

Conversion Factors

Example 3:

"A popular item at our local shop is Lumpy Sprout Ketchup (not available in all areas). The Extra Large Size is the most popular and weighs 2400 g. How much is this in kg?"

See page 88.

Step 1) Conversion Factor = 1000
(because 1 kg = 1000 g)

Step 2) 2400 × 1000 = 2 400 000 kg (Uulp..)
2400 ÷ 1000 = 2.4 kg (that's more like it)

Step 3) So the answer must be that 2400 g = 2.4 kg

Example 4:

"Toby, my pet elephant, weighs 12 tonnes.
How much does he weigh in kg?"

Step 1) Conversion Factor = 1000
(because 1 tonne = 1000 kg)

Step 2) 12 × 1000 = 12 000 kg (looks OK)
12 ÷ 1000 = 0.012 kg (that's a pretty light elephant)

Step 3) So the answer must be that 12 tonnes = 12 000 kg

You don't have the Conversion Factor. I thought it was very karaoke...

What a nice feeling — two lovely pages and just the 3 steps of the Conversion Factor method to learn. If you're reading this and you've still no idea what the Conversion Factor method is — look at all the big colourful boxes on the last two pages. Not only are they pretty, they'll help you with these...

1) Kevin the Sea-slug was found to weigh 0.16 tonnes. What is this in kg?
2) My little brother eats 32 ounces of Lumpy Sprout Ketchup per day.
What is this in pounds? (1 pound = 16 ounces).

Angles

Angles aren't that bad — you just have to learn them, that's all. And sometimes give them sweets.

The Four Types of Angle

1) Acute Angles

SHARP POINTY ONES:
(less than 90 degrees (90°))

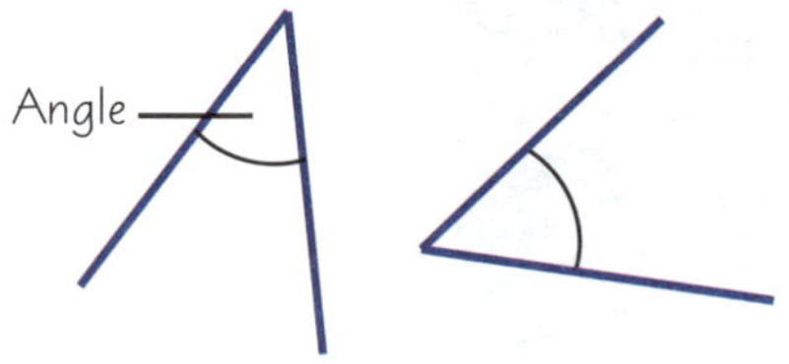

2) Obtuse Angles

FLATTER-LOOKING ONES:
(between 90° and 180°)

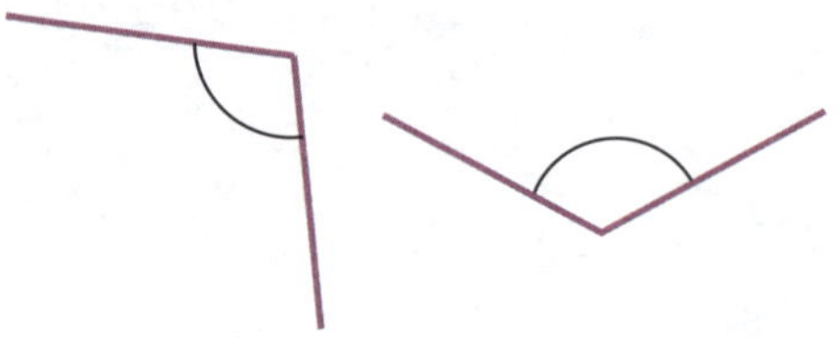

3) Reflex Angles

ONES THAT BEND BACK ON THEMSELVES:
(more than 180°)

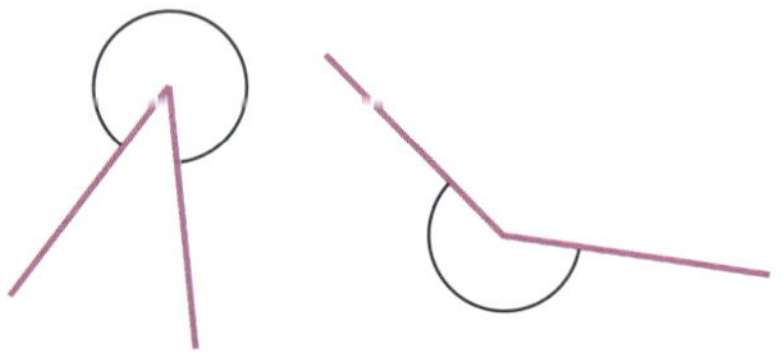

4) Right Angles

SQUARE CORNERS
(exactly 90°)

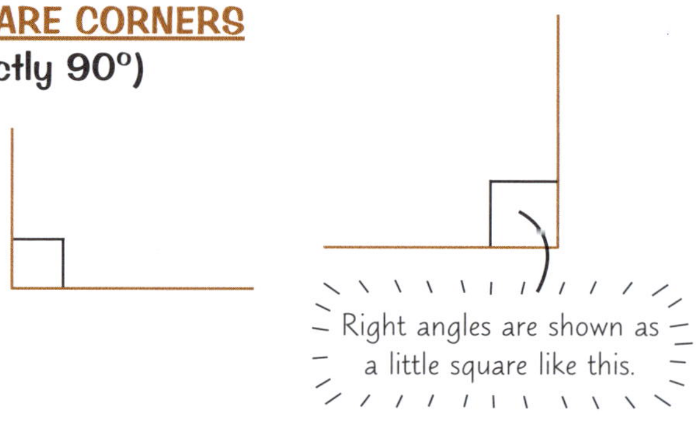

Angles Are Named Using Three Letters

1) In most angle questions, the diagram will have a letter next to each corner.
2) To say which angle you're talking about, use THREE of the letters.
3) The MIDDLE LETTER is the corner where the angle is.
4) The OTHER TWO LETTERS tell you WHICH TWO LINES are either side of the angle.

EXAMPLES:

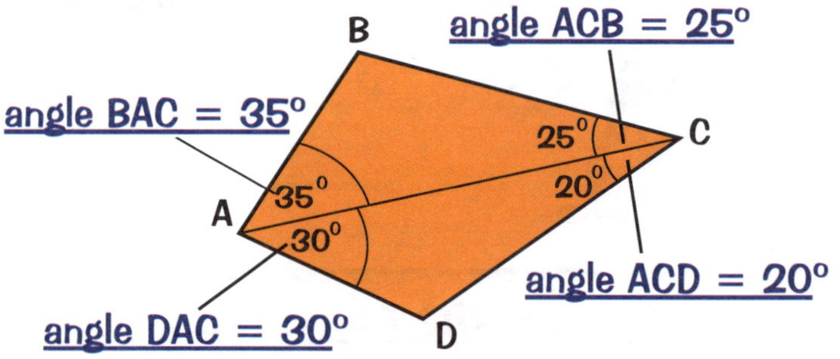

(NOT TO SCALE)

Roses are red, tulips are plum, if you were an angle you'd be acute one...

Ho, ho, ho — pretty funny aren't I. Anyway, moving on...

1) LEARN what ACUTE, OBTUSE, REFLEX and RIGHT ANGLES are. Draw one example of each.

Measuring Angles with Protractors

If you need to measure an angle, DON'T PANIC, just reach for your protractor and follow these tips.

Two Rules for Getting it Right

There are TWO REALLY IMPORTANT THINGS to watch out for when using a protractor:

1) ALWAYS put the 0° LINE at the START OF THE ANGLE.

2) CHECK you're reading from the RIGHT SCALE.

These scales won't work.

How To Measure An Angle:

1) ALWAYS position the protractor with the 0° line along the start line of the angle, as shown below:

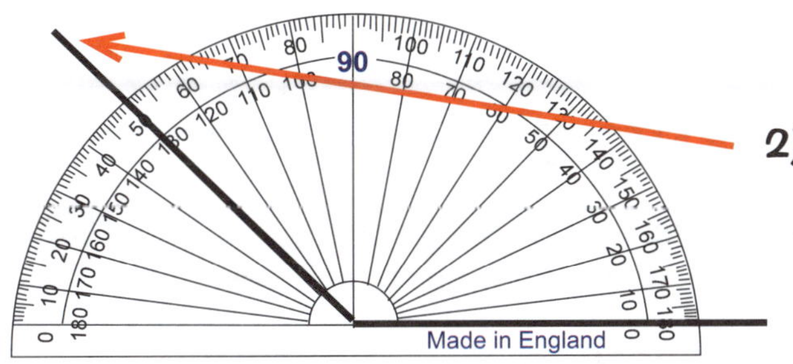

2) COUNT THE ANGLE IN 10° STEPS from the 0° line right round to the other one over there.

← Start line (0°)

3) BEFORE YOU READ A NUMBER OFF THE SCALE — check it's the RIGHT SCALE first, because there are TWO scales to choose from.

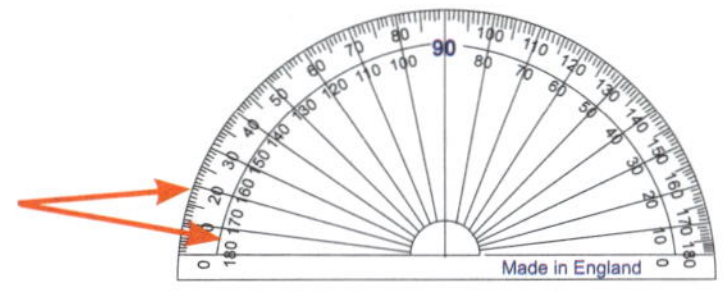

4) The answer here is 130° — NOT 50°. You should get this right if you start counting 10°, 20°, 30°, 40°, etc. from the start line until you reach the other line.

5) You could also estimate it as a check. It looks like an obtuse angle so it must be between 90° and 180° (see p.92) — which means 130° is the right number to pick.

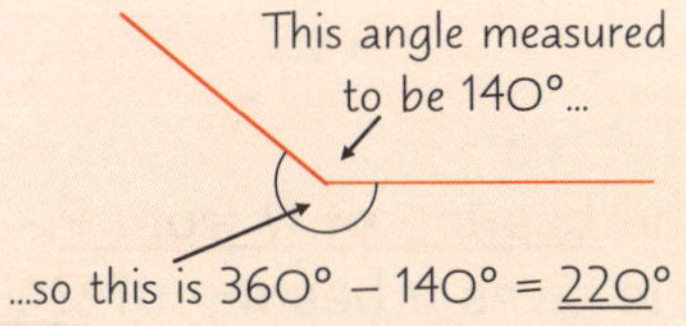

For reflex angles (see p.92) like this one — measure the angle on the OTHER SIDE then take it away from 360°.

Neither will these.

See how you measure up when it comes to angles...

...and have a go at these:

1) LEARN the 2 rules for using protractors. Close the book and say them to yourself.

2) Use a protractor to measure the angle on the right.

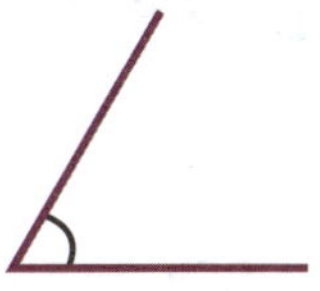

Compass Directions and Bearings

By the end of this page you should have got your bearings about bearings. Ahem.

The Eight Points Of the Compass

1) Make sure you know all these 8 DIRECTIONS ON THE COMPASS.
2) Remember the order of the main 4 going clockwise by saying: "Naughty Elephants Squirt Water".
3) For other directions (i.e. not exactly North or South or South-East, etc), you have to use BEARINGS.

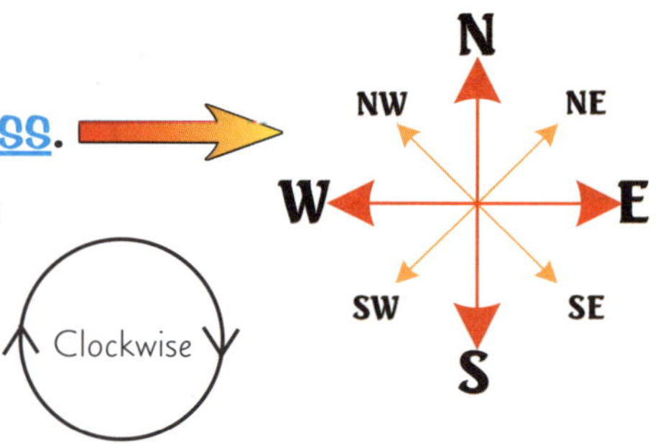

Bearings

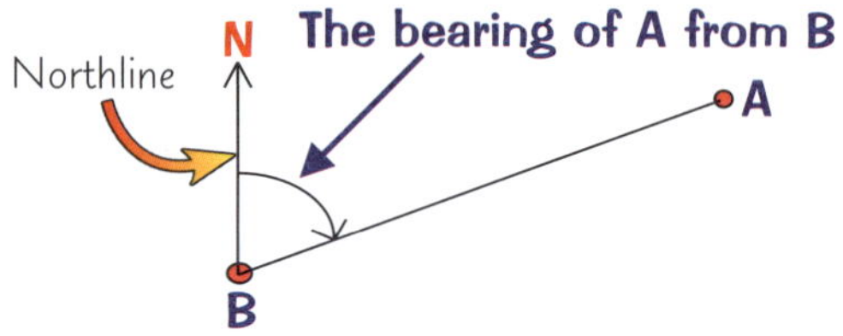

1) A bearing is a DIRECTION given as an ANGLE in degrees.
2) All bearings are measured CLOCKWISE from the NORTHLINE. (Just a line pointing North.)
3) All bearings are given as 3 figures: e.g. 060° rather than just 60°, 008° rather than 8°, etc.

The 3 Key Words For Bearings Questions

1) 'FROM' Find the word 'FROM' in the question, and put your pencil on the diagram at the point you are going 'from'.

You might need to draw a line between the two points if it's not already there.

2) NORTHLINE At the point you are going 'FROM', draw in a NORTHLINE.

3) CLOCKWISE Now draw in or measure the angle CLOCKWISE from the northline to the line joining the two points. This angle is the BEARING.

EXAMPLE: Find the bearing of Q from P:

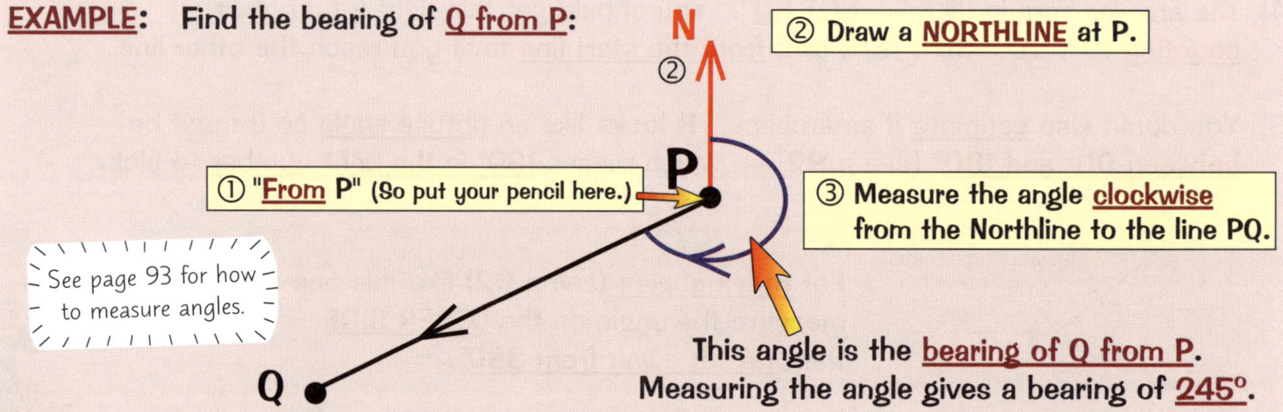

Compasses — we'd be lost without them...

Learn the eight points of a compass, and the 3 key words for bearings, and you'll be fine.

1) Draw a blob on a piece of paper to represent home, and then draw a line:
a) going out in a South-Westerly direction from home, and b) on a bearing of 080° from home.

Constructing Triangles

You need to know how to draw triangles <u>accurately</u> — which means <u>lengths and angles</u> being <u>exactly</u> what they're supposed to be.

When drawing shapes, <u>construct</u> means you have to draw them <u>accurately</u>.

Use a Ruler and Protractor to Draw Triangles

1) You'll be told <u>2 side lengths</u> of the triangle, and the <u>angle between them</u>.
2) You can draw the triangle using a <u>ruler</u>, a <u>protractor</u> and the <u>method below</u>.

Example: Construct triangle DEF. DE = 5 cm, DF = 3 cm, and angle EDF = 40°.

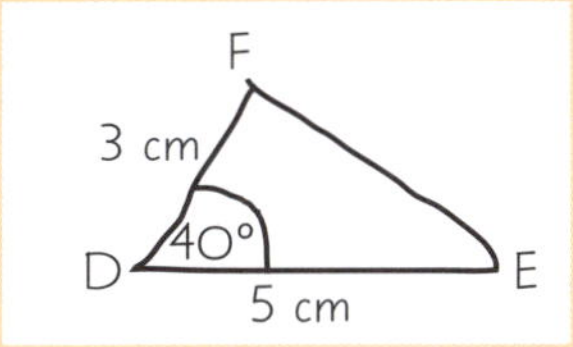

1) Roughly <u>sketch and label</u> the triangle.

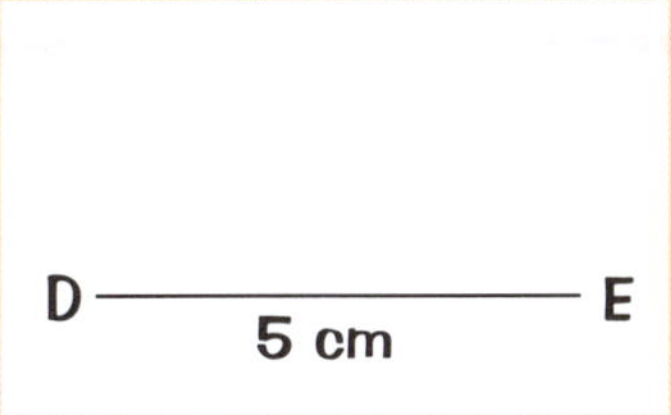

2) Draw the <u>base line</u> — here I've picked DE. Draw a <u>line</u> 5 cm long and <u>label</u> the ends D and E.

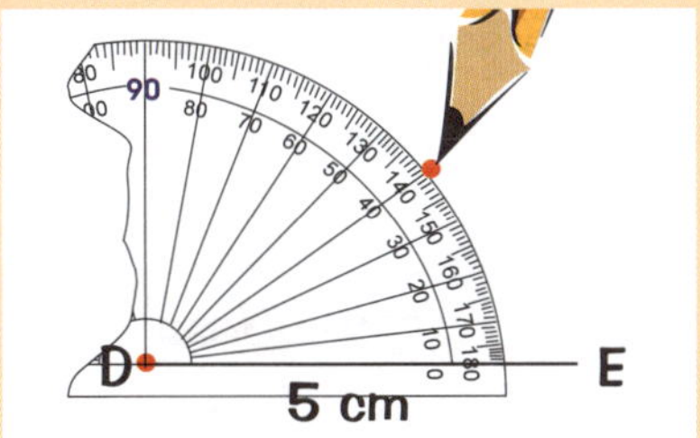

3) Next you have to <u>draw the angle EDF</u> at point D:
   - Place the <u>centre</u> of the protractor <u>over D</u>, with the <u>0° line level with DE</u>.
   - <u>Measure</u> 40° and put a <u>dot</u>, as shown.
   - <u>Join up</u> D and the dot with a <u>light</u> pencil line.

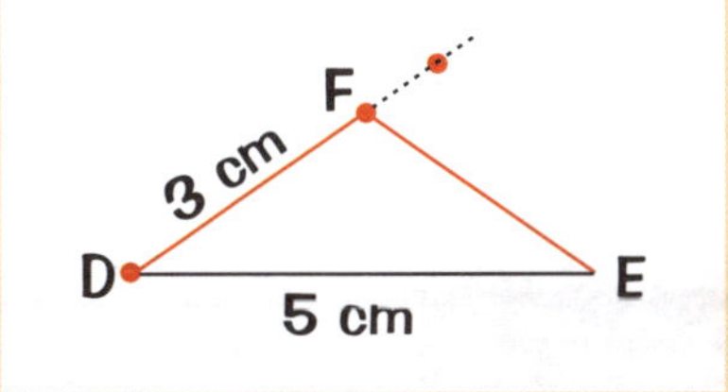

4) Measure <u>3 cm from D</u> on this light pencil line and put another dot, <u>labelled F</u>.
5) <u>Join up D and F</u> with a thicker line. Now you've drawn the <u>two sides</u> and the <u>angle</u>.
6) Finally, join up F and E to <u>complete</u> the triangle.

<u>DON'T</u> rub out your working lines and dots — these show you've done it properly. Make sure you do them lightly in the first place so it's not too messy.

Revision Test for Unit 3 — 2

1) What does it mean if two shapes are:
a) congruent, b) similar?

2) What transformation maps
a) shape A onto shape B?
b) shape C onto shape D?
c) shape C onto shape E?

Make sure you give all the details needed for each transformation.

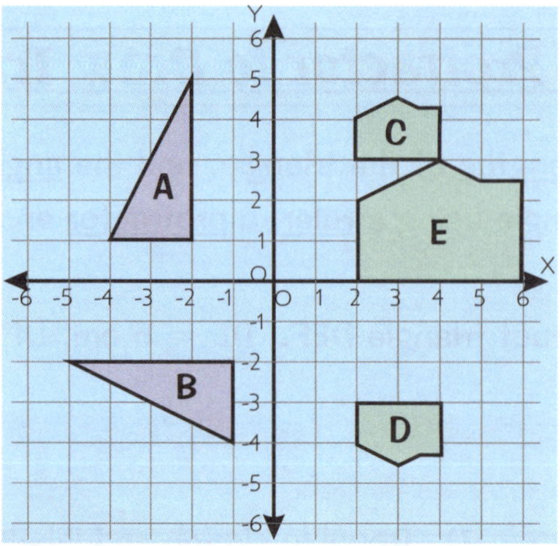

3) In a snail race, my pet Slimy finished the 2 metre race in 200 seconds.
What was his speed in metres per second (m/s)?

4) Jeb is planning a road trip. On the map his journey measures 12 cm.
If the map has a scale of 1 cm to 30 km, what is the real length of his journey in km?

5) Esther is drawing a scale plan of her bedroom, which is 6 m wide.
How wide will it be on the drawing if she uses a scale of 1 cm to 0.5 m?

6) Ali's pet worm is 6 cm long. How long is this in: a) millimetres, b) metres?

7) Jane is making pancakes. She has 0.7 litres of milk but the recipe says she needs 600 cm^3.
Does she have enough milk to make the pancakes?

8) Kylie is going on holiday and needs some spending money.
She wants to take $2400. How much is that in pounds (£), if £1 = $12?

This is the sign for dollars.

This is a conversion factor question.

9) Look at the diagram on the right, and say whether the following angles are acute, obtuse, reflex or right angles:
a) XYZ b) WZY
c) WXY d) XWZ

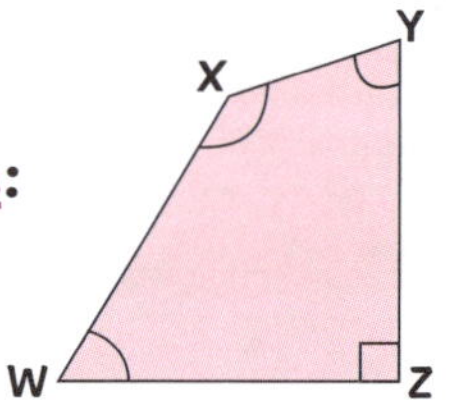

10) Draw a diagram showing the eight points of the compass.

11) A ship sets off from Port P on a bearing of 160°.
Show its direction on the drawing opposite:

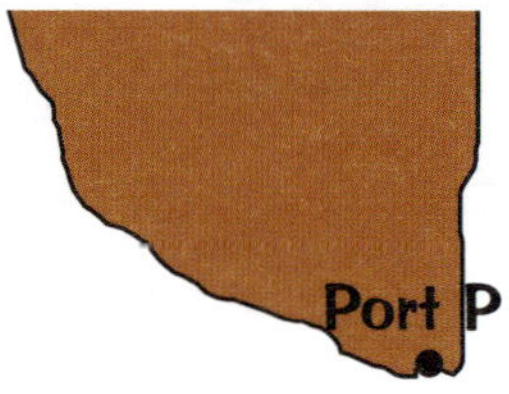

12) Construct a triangle ABC with sides AB = 9 cm,
AC = 10 cm and angle BAC = 50°.

Answers

Unit 1 — Statistics and Number

P.6 Rounding: 1) a) 3 **b)** 5 **c)** 2 **d)** 7 **e)** 3 **2) a)** 300 **b)** 500 **c)** 100 **3) a)** 5.4 **b)** 0.1

P.7 Fractions: 1) a) 5/6 **b)** 2/3 **2) a)** 20 **b)** 36

P.9 Percentages: 1) £27

P.10 Percentages: 1) 20%

P.12 Ratios: 1) 40p **2)** Recipe for 9: 9 rats, 4.5 toads, 18 potatoes and an even bigger bit of pastry.

P.14 Types of Data: 1) a) discrete **b)** qualitative **c)** qualitative **d)** continuous

P.15 Questionnaires: 1) a) "A lot of television" can mean different things to different people. **b)** This is a leading question. **c)** The answers to this question do not cover all the possible options.

P.17 Sampling: 1) Yes, it could be biased. It only has information from one year group and different year groups might have different music tastes.

P.19 Mode, Median, Mean and Range:
First, order the numbers: -14, -12, -5, -5, 0, 1, 3, 6, 7, 8, 10, 14, 18, 23, 25
Mean = 5.3, Median = 6, Mode = -5, Range = 39

P.25 Bar Charts: 1) See bar chart on the right.
P.27 Pie Charts: See pie chart below.

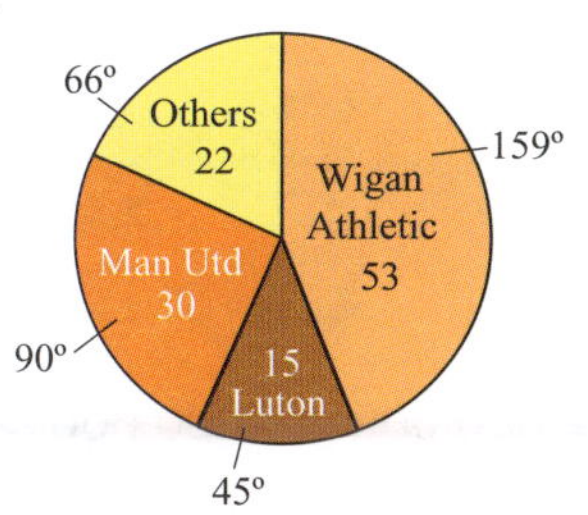

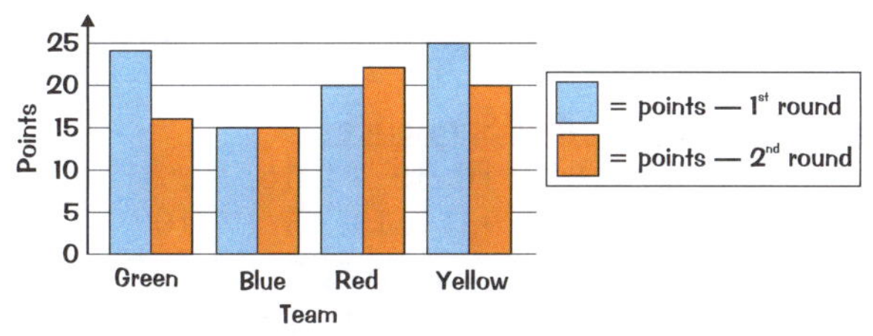

P.28 Probability: 1) a) likely **b)** $\frac{1}{4}$ (or 25% or 0.25)

P.29 Equal and Unequal Probabilities: 1) $\frac{1}{5}$ or 20% or 0.2

P.30 Listing Outcomes: 1) See right. **a)** 36 **b)** 5 **c)** P(8) = $\frac{5}{36}$

Dice 2 (columns), Dice 1 (rows)

	1	2	3	4	5	6
1	2	3	4	5	6	7
2	3	4	5	6	7	8
3	4	5	6	7	8	9
4	5	6	7	8	9	10
5	6	7	8	9	10	11
6	7	8	9	10	11	12

Revision Test for Unit 1 — 1

1) **a)** 1 **b)** 3 **c)** 16 **d)** 12 2) **a)** 250 **b)** 900 3) **a)** 5.3 **b)** 3.5 **c)** 6.2
4) **a)** E.g. 2/8 **b)** E.g. 4/10 **c)** E.g. 14/12 5) 12 6) 1/3 7) 1/4 8) **a)** 150 **b)** 160 9) £400
10) 56 11) **a)** £15 **b)** £315 12) 5% 13) 5:2 14) **a)** 2:5 **b)** 13:5 **c)** 2:3 15) £1.41

Revision Test for Unit 1 — 2

1) **a)** primary **b)** quantitative **c)** discrete
2) It's not clear what he means by "big", and also people might be too embarrassed to answer truthfully / it could be a sensitive question.
3) E.g. he could take a sample, and put the data into groups / classes.
4) First put in order: 2, 3, 4, 6, 7, 7, 12, 15 **a)** 7 **b)** 6.5 **c)** 7 **d)** 13
5) Pictogram, 35 angry customers. 6) No, the graph shows no correlation.
7) **a)** Angles are: Blue 108°, Red 135°, Yellow 36°, White 81°.
b) See pie chart to the right.

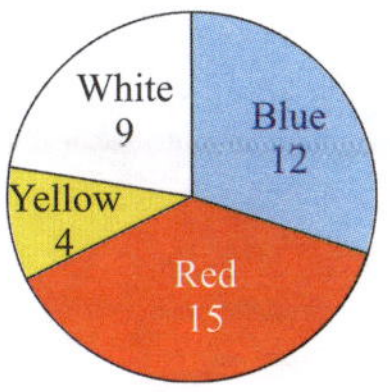

8) P(not 6) = 0.8 9) 20% 10) **a)** See right **b)** $\frac{1}{12}$

	1	2	3	4	5	6
Heads	H,1	H,2	H,3	H,4	H,5	H,6
Tails	T,1	T,2	T,3	T,4	T,5	T,6

Answers

Unit 2 — Number and Algebra

P.33 Ordering Numbers:

1) a) One million, two hundred and thirty-four thousand, five hundred and thirty-one
b) Twenty-three thousand, four hundred and fifty-six **c)** Two thousand, four hundred and fifteen
d) Three thousand, four hundred and two **e)** Two hundred and three thousand, four hundred and twelve
2) 56 421 **3)** 9, 23, 87, 345, 493, 1029, 3004 **4)** 0.008, 0.09, 0.1, 0.2, 0.307, 0.37

P.34 Addition and Subtraction: 1) a) 806 **b)** 186 **2) a)** 171 cm **b)** 19 cm

P.35 Adding and Subtracting Decimals: 1) a) £2.84 **b)** £2.16

P.36 Multiplying by 10, 100, etc: 1) a) 3450 **b)** 1230 **c)** 9650 **d)** 180 000

P.37 Dividing by 10, 100, etc: 1) a) 0.245 **b)** 6.542 **c)** 0.00308 **d)** 1.6

P.39 Dividing Without a Calculator: 1) 336 **2)** 616 **3)** 832 **4)** 17 976 **5)** 121 **6)** 12 **7)** 12 **8)** 25

P.40 Multiples, Factors and Primes:
1) 6, 12, 18, 24, 30, 36, 42, 48, 54, 60 and 7, 14, 21, 28, 35, 42, 49, 56, 63, 70
2) 1, 2, 3, 4, 6, 9, 12, 18, 36
3) 2, 3, 5, 7, 11, 13, 17, 19, 23, 29

P.42 Special Number Sequences:
1) EVENS: 2, 4, 6, 8, 10, 12, 14, 16, 18, 20
ODDS: 1, 3, 5, 7, 9, 11, 13, 15, 17, 19
SQUARES: 1, 4, 9, 16, 25, 36, 49, 64, 81, 100
CUBES: 1, 8, 27, 64, 125, 216, 343, 512, 729, 1000
POWERS OF 2: 2, 4, 8, 16, 32, 64, 128, 256, 512, 1024
POWERS OF 10: 10, 100, 1000, 10 000, 100 000, 1 000 000, 10 000 000, 100 000 000, 1 000 000 000, 10 000 000 000

2) a) 56, 134, 156, 36, 64 **b)** 23, 45, 81, 25, 97, 125 **c)** 81, 25, 36, 64 **d)** 125, 64 **e)** 64

P.44 Cube Roots: 1) +6 and –6 **2)** 3

P.45 Fractions, Decimals and Percentages: 1) a) 7/10 and 70% **b)** 1/100 and 1% **c)** 6/10 = 3/5 and 60%

P.46 Fractions: 1) a) 15/24 = 5/8 **b)** 32/35 **c)** 4/8 = 1/2 **d)** 2/5 **e)** 7/10 **2)** 2/3

P.47 Ratios: 1) 24 **2)** £1000:£1400

P.49 Negative Numbers: 1) a) +12 **b)** -6 **c)** -3 **d)** +1
P.50 Powers and Letters: 1) a) 3^4 **b)** 4^3 **c)** a^5 **d)** $3ab^2$ **e)** $7b^2$

P.52 Algebra — Brackets: 1) a) $4x + y - 4$ **b)** $9x + 5xy - 5$ **2) a)** $2x - 4$ **b)** $5x + x^2$ **c)** $y^2 + xy$ **d)** $6xy - 18y$

P.53 Formulas: 1) a) 25 **b)** 13 **c)** 5 **2)** A = 12

P.54 Making Formulas from Words: 1) y = 5x – 3 **2)** C = 95n

P.55 Solving Equations: 1) x = 2 **2)** x = 3

P.56 Solving Equations: 1) a) x = 6 **b)** q = 32 **c)** x = 4 **d)** y = 2

P.58 Number Patterns and Sequences: 1) a) 9 (subtract 2 from the previous term)
b) 22 (add one extra each time to the previous term) **c)** 200 000 (multiply the previous term by 10)
2) a) 1 (divide the previous term by 2) **b)** 125 (add the previous two terms)

P.59 X and Y Coordinates:
1) A(4, 5) B(6, 0) C(5, -5) D(0, -3) E(-5, -2) F(-4, 0) G(-3, 3) H(0, 5)

P.62 Straight-Line Graphs: 1) and **2)** See right.

x	-4	-2	-1	0	1	2	4
y	-6	-4	-3	-2	-1	0	2

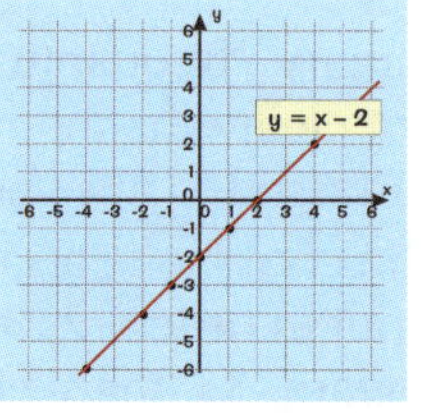

Answers

Revision Test for Unit 2 — 1

1) One million, three hundred and six thousand, five hundred and fifteen.
2) **a)** 2, 23, 45, 123, 132, 789, 2200, 6534 **b)** 0.0021, 0.003, 0.01, 0.05, 0.12, 0.6
3) **a)** 1145 **b)** 165 **c)** 11.13 4) **a)** £7.79 **b)** £2.21 5) £120 6) 32p 7) **a)** 759 **b)** 29
8) 10, 20, 30, 40, 50, 60 9) 1, 2, 3, 5, 6, 10, 15, 30 10) Square numbers are what you get when you multiply a number by itself, they are the areas of squares of side lengths 1, 2, 3, etc. The first five are: 1, 4, 9, 16, 25.
11) **a)** +15 and –15 **b)** 6 12) **a)** 0.4 **b)** 4/10 = 2/5 13) **a)** 4/15 **b)** 15/48 = 5/16 **c)** 7/8 **d)** 2/9
14) 7/8 15) £200:£600

Revision Test for Unit 2 — 2

1) **a)** +6 **b)** –32 **c)** –3 **d)** +5 2) **a)** $4n^3$ **b)** $2a^2$ 3) $5x + 3y$ 4) **a)** $12g + 20h - 4$ **b)** $x^2 - 6x$
5) **a)** $F = \frac{9}{5}C + 32$ **b)** 86 °F 6) x = +9 or –9 7) **a)** x = 4 **b)** x = 7 **c)** x = 9 **d)** x = –3
8) **a)** 19, 23; add 4 to the previous term **b)** 6, 3; subtract one less each time from the previous term
c) 48, 96; double the previous term **d)** 150, 75; halve the previous term
9) See graph on far right.

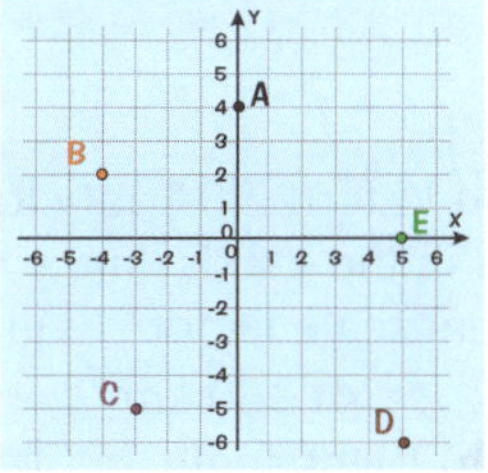

10) **a)**

x	-5	-3	-1	0	1	2	4	6
y	-2	0	2	3	4	5	7	9

b)

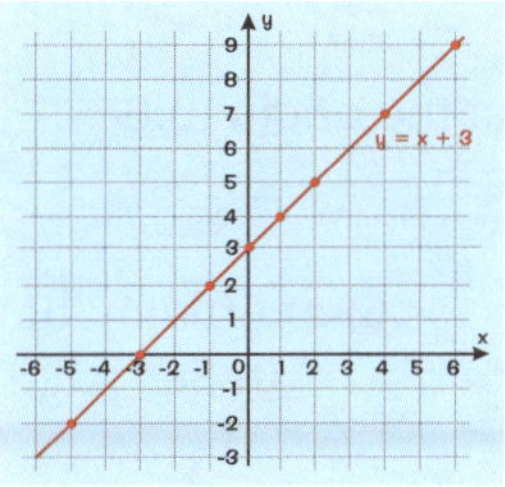

11) **a)** walking 1.5 km away at a steady speed
b) stopped **c)** 2.5 km
12) 30 chickens

Unit 3 — Geometry and Algebra

P.71 Regular Polygons:
1) A regular polygon is a many-sided shape where all the sides and angles are the same.
2) Equilateral triangle, square, regular pentagon, regular hexagon, regular heptagon, regular octagon
P.72 Perimeters: 1) Perimeter is the distance all the way around the outside of a shape. **2)** 42 cm
P.73 Areas: 1) 40 cm² **2)** 20 cm²
P.75 Volume: 1) 9 m³
P.78 Parallel and Perpendicular Lines: See right.

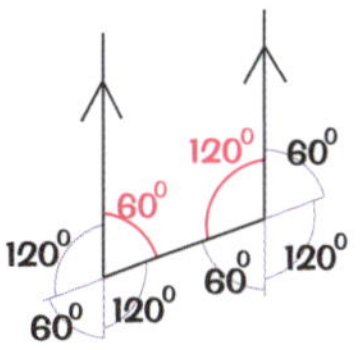

P.80 Congruence and Similarity: 1) a) i, ii and iv are similar.
b) i and ii are congruent.
P.84 The Four Transformations — Reflection:
1) A to B rotation ¼ turn (90°) clockwise about the origin (0,0).
B to C reflection in the line y=x.
C to A reflection in the y-axis (line x = 0).
A to D translation of 9 left and 7 down.
P.87 Maps and Map Scales: 1) 1400 m **2)** 3 cm
P.88 Metric and Imperial Units: 1) a) 200 **b)** 650 **2) a)** 2 **b)** 3 **3)** 4
P.91 Conversion Factors: 1) 160 kg **2)** 2 pounds (lbs)
P.93 Measuring Angles with Protractors: 2) 60°
P.94 Compass Directions and Bearings: 1) a) and **b)** See right.

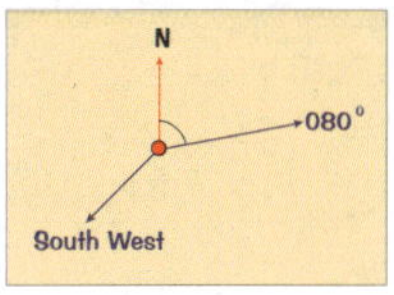

Answers

Revision Test for Unit 3 — 1

1) a) 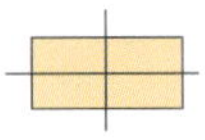 b) 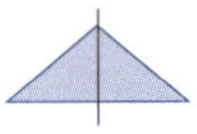 c) 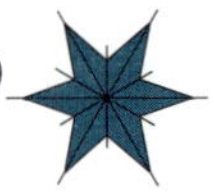

2) a) order 2 b) order 1 c) order 6
3) a) 4 cm b) They're the same size.
4) rhombus
5) See page 70. The triangular prism and the cylinder are prisms.
6) 8 sides, all the same length, 8 lines of symmetry, rotational symmetry order 8, all angles the same.
7) a) 3 m b) 32 m 8) 84 m^2 9) a) 18 cm^2 b) 36 cm^2 10) 37.7 cm 11) 5500 cm^3
12) 160° 13) X = 110°, Y = 40° 14) a) 100° b) Corresponding angles

Revision Test for Unit 3 — 2

1) See page 80
2) a) Rotation ¼ turn (90°) anticlockwise about the origin (0,0)
b) Reflection in the x-axis (line y = 0)
c) Enlargement scale factor 2 with centre (2,6)
3) 0.01 m/s 4) 360 km 5) 12 cm 6) a) 60 mm b) 0.06 m 7) Yes 8) £200
9) a) Acute b) Right angle c) Obtuse d) Acute 10) See page 94
11)

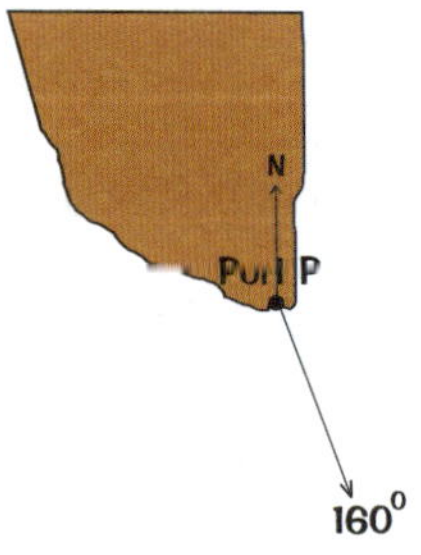

Index

Index